FORTRESS • 98

THE FORTIFICATIONS OF ANCIENT EGYPT 3000–1780 BC

CAROLA VOGEL

ILLUSTRATED BY BRIAN DELF
Series editor Marcus Cowper

First published in 2010 by Osprey Publishing
Midland House, West Way, Botley, Oxford OX2 0PH, UK
44-02 23rd St, Suite 219, Long Island City, NY 11101, USA
E-mail: info@ospreypublishing.com

ISBN: 978 1 84603 956 0
E-book ISBN: 978 1 84603 957 7

Editorial by Ilios Publishing Ltd, Oxford, UK (www.iliospublishing.com)
Cartography: Bounford.com
Design: Ken Vail Graphic Design, Cambridge, UK (kvgd.com)
Index by Michael Forder
Originated by PDQ Digital Media Solutions, Suffolk, UK
Printed in China through Bookbuilders

10 11 12 13 14   10 9 8 7 6 5 4 3 2 1

A CIP catalogue record for this book is available from the British Library.

FOR A CATALOGUE OF ALL BOOKS PUBLISHED BY OSPREY MILITARY AND AVIATION PLEASE CONTACT:

NORTH AMERICA
Osprey Direct, c/o Random House Distribution Center,
400 Hahn Road, Westminster, MD 21157
Email: uscustomerservice@ospreypublishing.com

ALL OTHER REGIONS
Osprey Direct, The Book Service Ltd, Distribution Centre, Colchester Road, Frating Green, Colchester, Essex, CO7 7DW
E-mail: customerservice@ospreypublishing.com

www.ospreypublishing.com

DEDICATION

To my friends in Israel who share my obsession with ancient Egypt: Dan'el, Deborah and Yossi.

ACKNOWLEDGEMENTS

To impart knowledge about a special subject in a concise way is a great task. It is with the support of my family, friends and colleagues that this book could be brightened up by a huge amount of images. Thus, special thanks for providing me with drawings, photographs or permissions are due to Dorothea Arnold, Verena Bach-Berkhahn, Brigitte Jaroš-Deckert, Miriam Lahitte, Franck Monnier, Greg Mumford, Daniel Polz, Miriam Reinemer, Stephan Seidlmeyer, Andreas Vogel and Pawel Wolf.

EDITOR'S NOTE

Unless otherwise indicated all images are part of the author's collection.

ARTIST'S NOTE

Readers may care to note that the original paintings from which the colour plates in this book were prepared are available for private sale. All reproduction copyright whatsoever is retained by the Publishers. All enquiries should be addressed to:

Brian Delf, 7 Burcot Park, Burcot, Abingdon, Oxon, OX14 3DH, UK

The Publishers regret that they can enter into no correspondence upon this matter.

THE FORTRESS STUDY GROUP (FSG)

The object of the FSG is to advance the education of the public in the study of all aspects of fortifications and their armaments, especially works constructed to mount or resist artillery. The FSG holds an annual conference in September over a long weekend with visits and evening lectures, an annual tour abroad lasting about eight days, and an annual Members' Day.

The FSG journal FORT is published annually, and its newsletter Casemate is published three times a year. Membership is international. For further details, please contact:
secretary@fsgfort.com
Website: www.fsgfort.com

THE HISTORY OF FORTIFICATION STUDY CENTRE (HFSC)

The History of Fortification Study Centre (HFSC) is an international scientific research organization that aims to unite specialists in the history of military architecture from antiquity to the 20th century (including historians, art historians, archaeologists, architects and those with a military background). The centre has its own scientific council, which is made up of authoritative experts who have made an important contribution to the study of fortification.

The HFSC's activities involve organizing conferences, launching research expeditions to study monuments of defensive architecture, contributing to the preservation of such monuments, arranging lectures and special courses in the history of fortification and producing published works such as the refereed academic journal *Questions of the History of Fortification*, monographs and books on the history of fortification. It also holds a competition for the best publication of the year devoted to the history of fortification.

The headquarters of the HFSC is in Moscow, Russia, but the centre is active in the international arena and both scholars and amateurs from all countries are welcome to join. More detailed information about the HFSC and its activities can be found on the website: www.hfsc.3dn.ru
E-mail: ciif-info@yandex.ru

THE WOODLAND TRUST

Osprey Publishing are supporting the Woodland Trust, the UK's leading woodland conservation charity, by funding the dedication of trees.

CONTENTS

THE FORTIFICATIONS OF ANCIENT EGYPT 3000–1780 BC

INTRODUCTION

This book seeks to shed light on Egypt's early military architecture by discussing its development from the first known fortified structures (*c*.3500–3300 BC) into an elaborate fortification system at the end of the Middle Kingdom (*c*.1780 BC).

Geographical features – Kemet: the black land

The question of Egypt's fortresses cannot be separated from that of its frontiers. The traditional borders of Egypt were the north-eastern Delta/Sinai, the Western Desert, the Mediterranean coast and the first Nile cataract at modern Aswan.

Throughout history Egypt has taken advantage of its distinct natural conditions. The regular Nile floods have defined its economic growth and cultural development. When, following these floods, the Nile withdrew to its riverbed it left behind fertile mud and created a stretch of easily cultivable land between the first cataract at modern Aswan and the Mediterranean coast. Therefore, it comes as no surprise that the ancient Egyptians named their country 'Kemet' – the black land – referring to the colour of this fertile mud. To the east and the west, the narrow Nile Valley and Delta were bounded by deserts, forming natural barriers that – for most of the period in question – isolated and protected Egypt from outside attack.

At some point in the 4th millennium BC two different agricultural powers evolved in the region: the Nagada culture (with its centre at Hierakonpolis) in the south and the Maadi culture in the north. Archaeological evidence shows traces of the Nagada culture appearing in the north as well, testifying to its growing influence. The question of how exactly a centralized state emerged in Egypt by 3050 BC is debated through to the current day. What is clear is that we know from various sources that Lower and Upper Egypt were unified and ruled by a king who wore the so-called Double-Crown, symbolizing

Aswan at the first cataract. Viewed from the open air area of the Nubian Museum situated in the south of the city. The building in the front is a reconstructed Nubian mud-brick house as used up to the present day. Behind this lies the Islamic cemetery amongst the lumps of granite.

the kingship's two different roots (the Red Crown stands for Lower Egypt, the White Crown for Upper Egypt). It is from this point onwards that we have increasing evidence of Egypt's natural borders being strengthened with forts.

Sources

For the time frame being covered (*c.*3000–1780 BC), a huge amount of sources allows us to reconstruct the development of the ancient Egyptian fortification system. Thanks to Egypt's dry climate, even organic material has survived over thousands of years in the desert sands. The following sources have been considered in this study:

View from Aswan to the island of Elephantine.

- The archaeological remains, foremost the mud-brick fortresses and findings discovered within them
- Rock inscriptions found in the neighbourhood of fortifications
- Papyri containing valuable information, e.g. a list with the propagandist names of 17 fortresses (*Ramesseum Onomasticon*), or a document describing the fortresses' monitoring tasks (Semna dispatches, Papyrus Berlin 10495)
- Models of towers or fortified structures
- Labels showing towers or fortresses
- Palettes depicting walled towns
- Tomb paintings depicting Egyptian or Asiatic fortresses in siege warfare
- Boundary stelae claiming to define Egypt's 'ends'
- Titles and ranks referring to members of garrisons
- Texts containing information about siege warfare

A chronology of fortification development

These sources will be combined to give a concise, chronological overview of the development of the ancient Egyptian fortifications from the earliest times to the highest point in their development in the Middle Kingdom.

A predynastic clay model from a tomb in Abadiyeh is thought to be the first evidence for an Egyptian fortress (*c.*3500–3200 BC). The item shows two men

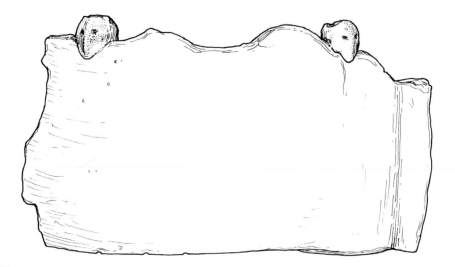

Predynastic clay model from a tomb in Abadiyeh, Ashmolean Museum, Oxford, E. 3202. This unique clay model is thought to be the first evidence for an Egyptian fortress (*c.*3500–3200 BC). The item, approximately 10cm high, shows two men peering over a crenellated wall. After J. C. Payne, *Catalogue of the Predynastic Egyptian Collection in the Ashmolean Museum*, Oxford, 2000, fig. 6, top.

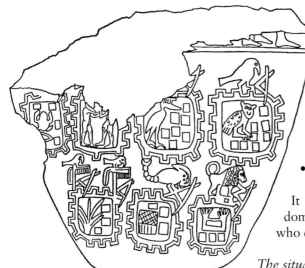

peering over a crenellated wall. Some 100 years later representations and models of towers and fortifications crop up more frequently, testifying to the measures taken by the recently unified Egyptian state in order to protect its people and goods. The appearance of single towers can be explained by two main needs:

- to guard the huge royal domains that produced the oil, vine and wheat for the Pharaoh's elaborate burial equipment,
- and to monitor the trouble spots along trade routes.

It is only natural that the products of the royal domains were of great interest to those nomadic tribes who existed on the margins of Egyptian society.

The situation in the north-east/Sinai

From the period of the Old Kingdom onwards various sources testify that the eastern Delta and parts of the Sinai were protected by fortresses to prevent an invasion along the coastal route from the Levant. In his tomb at Giza (G 4970, Western Cemetery) the official Nesutnefer (early 5th Dynasty) proudly names his military titles. Among them appears the title 'Overseer of fortified enclosures, overseer of the deserts, overseer of the royal fortresses in the 13th lower Egyptian *nome* [administrative district]'. As the latter was located in the north-eastern Delta, Nesutnefer seems to have been in charge of one of the most sensitive regions in the whole of Egypt. In addition to epigraphic and pictorial evidence, the archaeological remains of an Old Kingdom fortress have been investigated only recently. At Ras Budran (South Sinai), a round fortress, made of roughly

Lower part of a famous ceremonial palette (the so-called 'Towns' or Tjehenu palette), Egyptian Museum, Cairo, CG 14238/JE 27434. The main scene, probably a battle, has been lost. The remaining lower part shows seven fortified settlements being attacked by various creatures symbolizing royal and divine power. The emblems like the lion, scorpion and falcon are using hoes in order to breach the walls. The palette might commemorate a series of victories in the northward expansion of the early kingdom of Hierakonpolis (*c.*3100 BC). After W. M. F. Petrie, *Ceremonial slate palettes and corpus of proto-dynastic pottery*, London, 1953, pl. G.

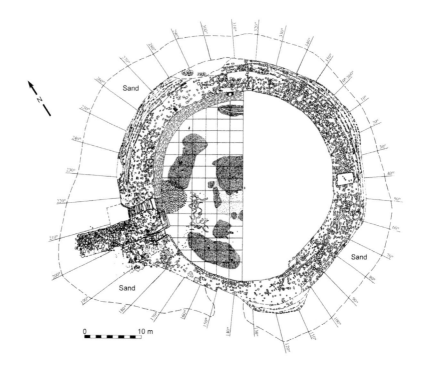

Plan of the round-shaped Old Kingdom limestone fort at Ras Budran, South Sinai. (© G. Mumford)

hewn stone, was discovered – the first Old Kingdom fortress known about in this region.

Another military installation built in order to protect Egypt's eastern border is known by epigraphic evidence only: the so-called 'Ways of Horus'. As it is only mentioned once in the Old Kingdom context, there is not enough evidence to decide whether this name refers to an individual site or a chain of fortresses like its more famous New Kingdom namesake. However, its significance seems to have increased in the Middle Kingdom where it is perodically mentioned. From at least the reign of Amenemhat I (1991–1962 BC) onwards the eastern delta was secured by a further fortification known as the 'Walls of the Ruler'. Like the Ways of Horus its importance within the Middle Kingdom defence system is undisputed, though its original appearance and possible location is still a matter for debate. The main question is, as with the Ways of Horus, whether the Walls of the Ruler named a string of fortresses or a single feature.

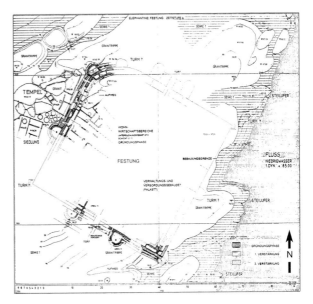

On the island of Elephantine archaeologists have found Egypt's oldest fortress guarding the country's southern border to Nubia. The square feature measures 51 by 51m (167 x 167ft) and dates back to the 1st Dynasty (c.3000 BC). Following various changes and improvements, Elephantine developed into a fortified town stretching over the southern part of the island.

The situation in the west

We have only scant knowledge about the situation on Egypt's western borders. We are nevertheless aware that throughout history the Egyptians have been troubled by Libyan tribes who have invaded the country repeatedly from the north-west. Early evidence of this comes from a ceremonial palette, the so-called 'Towns' or Tjehenu (= Libyan) palette. Though the main scene, probably a battle, has been lost, the remaining lower part shows seven fortified settlements being attacked by various creatures symbolizing royal and divine power. The emblems – lion, scorpion and falcon – are using hoes in order to breach the walls. The palette might commemorate a series of victories in the north-westward expansion of the Early Kingdom of Hierakonpolis (c.3100 BC) and its clashes with Libyan forces.

Some 100 years later clear evidence about the need to protect Egyptian settlements in the western regions arrives from the Dakhla Oasis. Here, at modern Ayn Asil, a huge fortified Old Kingdom town has been discovered, testifying that the governors of the town were forced to strengthen their isolated settlement in order to protect their belongings. Obviously, the wealth of the site was of great interest to marauding groups, most likely coming from the Libyan Desert.

Rock drawing from Gebel Sheik Suleiman (second cataract). Drawing after W. B. Emery, *Egypt in Nubia*, London, 1965, p. 126.

Egypt showing the locations of ancient and modern sites

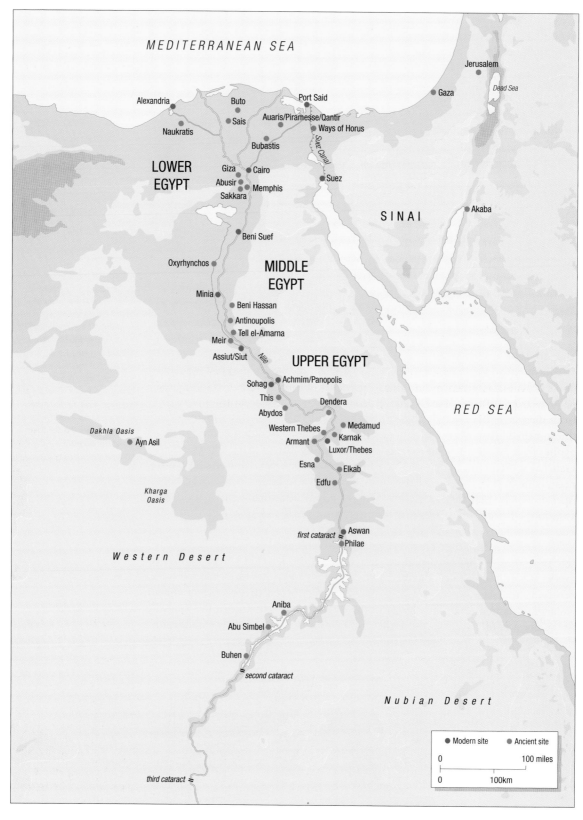

MEDITERRANEAN SEA

Jerusalem

Dead Sea

Gaza

Alexandria

Buto

Port Said

Sais

Auaris/Piramesse/Qantir

Ways of Horus

Naukratis

Bubastis

Suez Canal

LOWER EGYPT

Giza

Cairo

Abusir

Memphis

Sakkara

Suez

SINAI

Akaba

Beni Suef

Oxyrhynchos

MIDDLE EGYPT

Minia

Beni Hassan

Antinoupolis

Tell el-Amarna

Meir

Nile

Assiut/Siut

UPPER EGYPT

Sohag

Achmim/Panopolis

This

Dendera

Abydos

RED SEA

Dakhla Oasis

Western Thebes

Medamud

Ayn Asil

Armant

Karnak

Luxor/Thebes

Esna

Elkab

Edfu

Kharga Oasis

first cataract

Aswan

Philae

Western Desert

Aniba

Abu Simbel

Buhen

second cataract

Nubian Desert

● Modern site   ● Ancient site

0   100 miles

0   100km

third cataract

Reconstruction of the Old Kingdom limestone fort at Ras Budran, South Sinai. The seashore, less than 200m (650ft) from the military installation, can be seen in the background. (© G. Mumford)

The situation in the south

From the very earliest years of the period in question, Pharaonic interest was directed towards the territory south of the first cataract of the Nile. Therefore, it does not come as a surprise that Egypt's earliest fortress (1st Dynasty) has been found precisely here, on the island of Elephantine.

Moreover, the first official testimony demonstrating Egypt's interest in ancient Nubia is given by an amazing rock drawing dated to the reign of King Djer (*c.*3000 BC, 1st Dynasty). It is thought to illustrate the first slave raid in Nubian history. The king came at least as far as the second cataract of the Nile, where he obviously wanted to commemorate his assumed success against the Nubians by carving the item. The drawing found on a rock called Gebel Sheik Suleiman shows a bound captive tied to the prow of the king's boat. The accompanying semi-pictographic text seems to celebrate the operation. The block was rescued from the floods of Lake Nasser and can be seen in the open air area of the National Museum in Khartoum.

The fortified town of Ayn Asil in the Dahkla Oasis. Whereas our knowledge about the system of fortifications in the Nile Valley is well founded, we lack information about the military defences in the western and eastern deserts. However, at least one site, the recently researched fortified Old Kingdom town in the Dahkla Oasis, proves the idea of fortifying remote spots. This view looks over the sanctuaries of the governors and remains of the settlement.

Wooden tablet depicting an early watch tower, London BM EA 35525. The item comes from the royal cemetery at Abydos and shows one of the oldest representations of watch towers. After W. M. Petrie, *The Royal Tombs of the Earliest Dynasties*, Pt. 2, EEF 21, London 1901, pl. 5.

Later sources demonstrate that, even though Nubia's valuable resources (human, animal and mineral) were exploited to a high degree, the country wasn't permanently occupied throughout the Old Kingdom period. The indigenous population, the so-called late A-Group culture, seemed to be a negligible force that could be controlled from the Egyptian motherland. So, peaceful trade-relations between the regions were possible.

The situation changed with the appearance of the so-called C-Group culture in Nubia, which can be traced from the 6th Dynasty onwards in Lower Nubia. The new assertiveness of this culture can be seen in the measures taken against them by the Pharaohs of the 11th and 12th Dynasty. Inscriptions record not only the massacre of rebels in Lower Nubia (Wawat), but also the destruction of their livelihood. At Korosko, rock inscription No. 73 reads '... I sailed downstream plucking corn and cutting down their remaining trees.' The intention seems quite clear: the complete physical and psychological destruction of the enemy.

During the reign of Senusret I, Egypt realized that to ensure a lasting control over Lower Nubia – and above all to guarantee unhindered access to Nubia's gold mines as well as resources deeper in the south – it would be necessary to build permanent fortifications.

Out of all the archaeological remains only Buhen, situated at the northern end of the second cataract, can be dated safely back to the early years of the reign of Senusret I. Structural parallels at phase I of Aniba, Kubban and Ikkur allow us to ascribe their construction to his reign as well. These fortifications situated on the bank of the Nile show a rectangular layout. Their ramparts were surrounded by wide ditches, which were protected by separate walls that ran parallel to the curtain. Those ditch-defences were further strengthened with horse-shoe-shaped bastions that projected into the ditch in the fashion of a modern caponier.

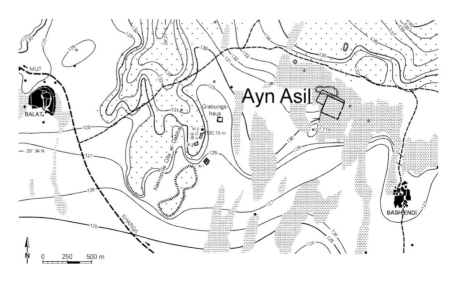

Map showing the location of Ayn Asil in the Dakhla Oasis. After J. Willeitner.

The fortress of Mirgissa, a complex of numerous buildings, including a unique preserved slipway for loads and ships in order to bypass the cataract, was most likely built by Senusret II.

During the reign of Senusret III the existing fortifications were intensively upgraded and new ones were built. In the region of the second cataract the following fortifications can be traced back to his reign: Semna-South, Semna-West, Kumma, Uronarti, Shalfak, Askut and Serra-East. The reason for this intensified military commitment might have been the increasing pressure brought about by the rise of the state of Kerma. This kingdom, whose centre was located at the third cataract, might have stretched as far as the area beyond Kurgus in the direction of the fifth cataract. Kerma's development into a complex and powerful state in Upper Nubia, conflicted tremendously with Egpypt's economic interests. As far as we can tell, writing does not seem to have been used in the kingdom of Kerma.

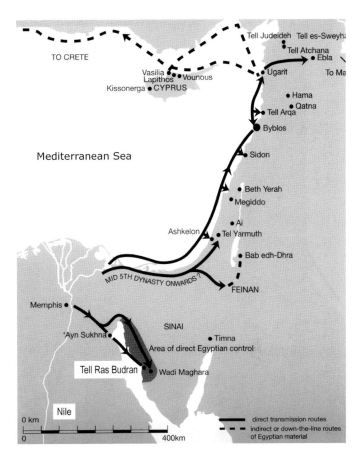

Map of the Egyptian Delta, Palestine and Syria showing the location of Ras Budran.
After K. N. Sowada, *Egypt in the Eastern Mediterranean during the Old Kingdom. An Archaeological Perspective.* OBO 237, (Freiburg (CH), 2009), fig. 47.

However, seals or their impressions found at control posts in the ancient town of Kerma prove that a highly developed adminstrative system existed, providing the basis for a complex commercial network. There is no doubt that Kerma developed slowly but steadily into an equal opponent for Egypt. Within the so-called Middle Kerma period, 2050–1750 BC – a time frame almost identical to that of the Egyptian Middle Kingdom – the erection of fortified walls, palaces and huge tombs is testified. Obviously, the Nubians, known to be perceptive warriors and gifted archers, took care to protect themselves from enemy raids. They built trenches, palisades and strong enclosure walls, strengthened with numerous bastions.

A thorough investigation of the Kerma culture has only just begun, but researchers such as Charles Bonnet and Matthieu Honegger from the University of Geneva have already conducted numerous surveys and excavations in order to enrich our knowledge on this important indigenous culture of ancient Nubia. Kerma's name derives from that of the modern city located south of the third cataract, on the east bank of the Nile, where the kingdom's capital and its eastern necropolis were found by the American scholar George A. Reisner during his excavations in the early 20th century.

Its inhabitants earned their living by farming (bovines and caprines), the exploitation of vegetable resources as well as hunting and fishing. Moreover, the trading of valuables such as gold, precious stones, ivory, animal hide, ebony and cattle contributed to the city's wealth. Kerma's location at the centre of a fertile basin and at the crossroads of desert routes linking Egypt, the Red Sea and Inner Africa was well chosen and supported its development.

The fortification walls of the early settlement on Elephantine.

Against this background, Egypt's goal was no longer to secure trading routes within C-Group territory, especially at the crossroads leading to the goldmines, but also to build a staggered defensive system against the rulers of Kerma. Because of this buffer zone it became possible to protect the traditional southern Egyptian border – the region around the first cataract – close to present-day Aswan. The expansion of the country's border to the second cataract – where the fortifications of Semna-West, Kumma and Semna-South protected the region of Batn el-Haggar against threats from the south – was so unfamiliar to the Egyptians that they referred to Semna-West as 'Southern-Elephantine'.

The famous boundary stela from Semna-West and its counterpart from Uronarti confirm that the fortresses, which clustered around the southern part of the second cataract, were considered as a true frontier, at least by the occupying power:

> Horus: Divine of Forms,
> Two Ladies: Divine of Manifestations,
> Dual King: Khakaure given life,
> Golden Horus: Being,
> Re's Bodily son, whom he loves,
> The Lord of the two lands: Senusret,
> given life, stability, power for all time!
> Year 16, month 3 of Peret (= Winter season):
> His Majesty made the southern boundary at Hech (region of Semna).
>
> I have made My boundary, out-southing my forefathers.
> I have exceeded what was handed down to me.
> I am a king, whose speaking is acting;
> what happens by my hand is what my heart plans;

Ancient Nubia, showing the chain of Middle Kingdom fortifications

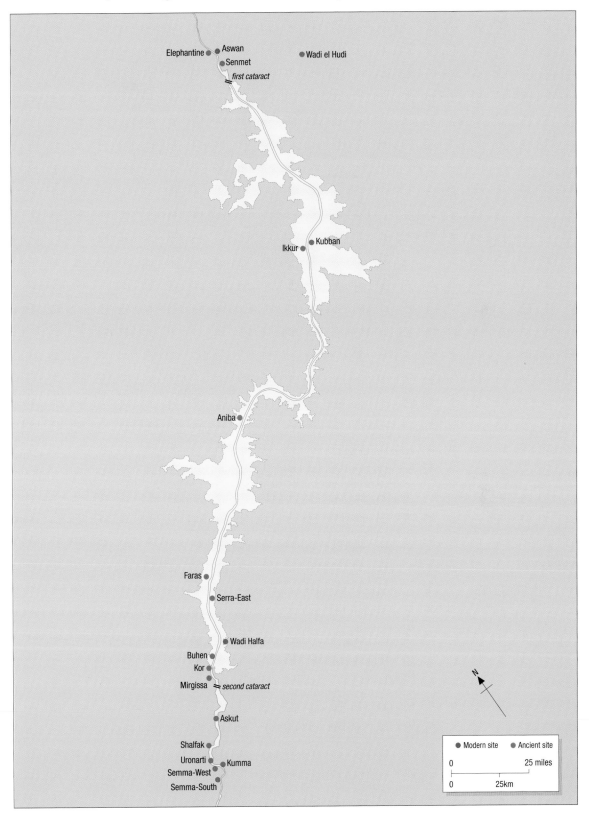

Elephantine • Aswan
• Senmet
first cataract

• Wadi el Hudi

Ikkur • • Kubban

Aniba •

Faras •
• Serra-East
• Wadi Halfa
Buhen •
Kor •
Mirgissa • second cataract

• Askut

Shalfak •
Uronarti •
Semma-West • Kumma
Semma-South

Modern site Ancient site
0   25 miles
0   25km

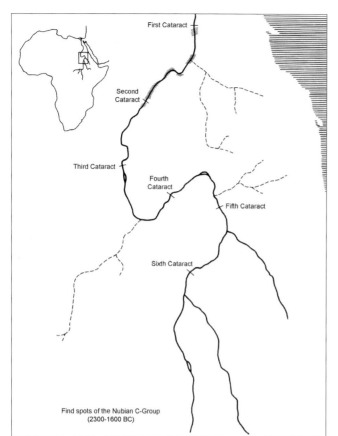

Find spots of the Nubian C-Group
(2300–1600 BC)

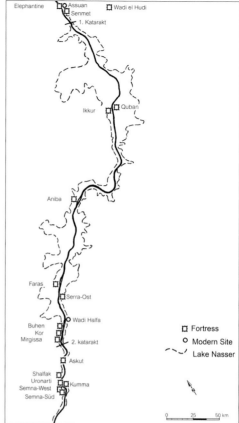

ABOVE LEFT

C-Group sites in Nubia. The hatched sections give the locations of major C-Group settlements between the First and Second Cataracts. After D. Wildung, *Sudan. Antike Königreiche am Nil*, Tübingen, 1996, fig. on p. 50.

ABOVE RIGHT

Map of Nubian fortresses. A point worth noting is the reduction in distance between individual fortresses the further one goes south, ending in a conglomeration of fortresses at the second cataract.

one who is aggressive to capture,
swift to success,
who sleeps not with a matter (still) in his heart;
who takes thought for the dependants, and stands by mercy;
who is unmerciful to the enemy that attacks him;
who attacks when attacked,
and is quiet when he is quiet;
who responds to a matter as it happens.

For he who is quiet after attack,
He is making the enemy's heart strong.
Aggression is bravery;
retreat is vile.
He who is driven from his boundary is a true back-turner,
answering him makes him retreat.
One is aggressive to him and he shows his back;
retreat and he becomes aggressive.
Not people to be respected –
they are wretches, broken-hearted!
My person has seen it – it is not an untruth,
For I have plundered their women, and carried off their underlings,
gone to their wells, driven off their bulls,
torn up their corn, and put fire to it.
As my father lives for me,

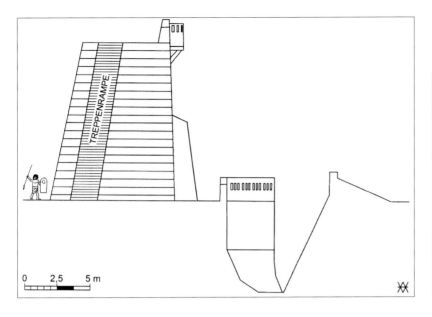

I speak true;
Here is no boastful phrase
Which has come to my mouth.
Now, as for any son of mine who shall maintain this boundary My Majesty has made, he is a son of mine who was born to My Majesty,
The son who vindicates his father is a model,
Making firm the boundary of his begetter.
But as for whoever shall abandon it, and who will not fight for it, he is no son of mine, and was not born to me!
My Majesty has had a statue of My Majesty set up on this boundary which My Majesty has made so that you might be inspired by it, and fight on behalf of it.
(Translation after R. B. Parkinson).

Another document also illustrates the Pharaonic idea of propaganda. A papyrus, the so-called *Ramesseum Onomasticon* (Papyrus Berlin 10495), has survived on which 17 fortresses situated between Gebel es Silsila in Upper Egypt and Semna-South at the second cataract are listed with their ancient Egyptian names. The names for those installations, which date back to the reign of Senusret III, the Middle Kingdom Pharaoh with the most agressive interest in penetrating Nubia, show a regular pattern containing

ABOVE LEFT
Cross-section of an ideal Nubian defence. (© A. Vogel)

ABOVE RIGHT
Boundary stela from Semna-West. After C. Obsomer, *Les campagnes de Sésostris III dans Hérodote*, Brussels, 1989, p. 182.

BELOW
Reconstruction of Semna-West after L. Borchardt. This view of the fortress is shown from the north-west. As the original appearance of the upper parts of the building is unknown, Borchardt based his reconstruction mainly on contemporary wall paintings, resulting in the adoption of small bartizans, resting on wooden beams.

	Fortress of…	Egyptian name	Transliteration/Translation	Identification after Gardiner	Identification after the author
1			D3jr-Stj Conqueror of Nubia	Semna-South	Semna-South
2			Shm-ḫʿw-k3.w-Rʿ.w m3ʿ-ḫrw Senusret III, justified	Semna-West	Semna-West
3			ʾItnw-pd.wt The one, who is resistant to the Bowmen	Kumma	Kumma
4			Hsf-ʾIwn.tjw Repelling the Iuntiu = the Nubian troglodytes/tribesmen	Uronarti	Uronarti
5			Wʿf-ḫ3s.wt To conquer the foreign countries	Shalfak	Shalfak
6			D3jr-Wtjw/ Dr Stj.w	Mirgissa	Askut
7			ʾIqn	Dabnarti	Mirgissa
8			Bwhn Buhen	Buhen	Buhen
9			ʾInq-t3.wj To combine the two countries	Sarret el-gharb, Wadi Halfa East(?)	Faras
10			Hsf-Md3.jw Repelling the Medjau	Sarret el-gharb, Faras	Serra-East
11			Mjʿm Miam	Aniba	Aniba
12			B3kj Baki	Kubban	Kubban
13			Zn-mw.t	Bigeh	Plain of Shellal
14			3bw 'of the Elephant'	Elephantine	Elephantine
15			…dd…	Between Elephantine and Silsila	Between Elephantine and Silsila
16				Between Elephantine and Silsila	Between Nos. 15 and 16
17			Hnj Hnj	Silsila	Silsila

a bellicose announcement against those enemies to which the fortress was most likely directed: e.g. *Ḥsf Ỉwn.tjw* for the fortress of Uronarti 'Repelling the Iuntiu = the Nubian troglodytes/tribesmen'. The table opposite gives their name in Hieroglyphic writing, a translation, the identification of the fortress after Sir A. Gardiner, and the identification of the fortress according to the author.

CHRONOLOGY

All dates BC

Predynastic Egypt

Badari	5500–4000
Naqada I (Amratien)	4000–3500
Naqada II	3500–3182
Naqada III/Dynasty 0	3182–3032

Protodynastic Egypt

1st Dynasty	3032–2853
2nd Dynasty	2853–2707

Old Kingdom

3rd Dynasty	2707–2639
4th Dynasty	2639–2504
5th Dynasty	2504–2347
6th Dynasty	2347–2216
7th Dynasty	70 days (misconception of Manetho)
8th Dynasty	17 kings *c.*2216–2170

First Intermediate Period

9th/10th Dynasty	
Rulers at Herakleopolis, 18 kings	*c.*2170–2020

Middle Kingdom

11th Dynasty	
Thebes, later entire Egypt	2119–1976
Mentuhotep II	2046–1995
12th Dynasty	
Amenemhet I	1976–1947
Senusret I	1956–1911/10
Amenemhet II	1914–1879/76
Senusret II	1882–1872
Senusret III	1872–1853/52
Amenhet III	1853–1806/05
Amenhet IV	1807/1806–1798/97
Nefrusobek	1798/97–1794/93

Painted pottery bowl from the rock tombs at Qubbet el-Hawa/Aswan, *c.*2200 BC. Egyptian artists frequently depicted hounds as companions of hunters and soldiers. The efficient use of these animals in such an environment ment that they needed to be trained.

DESIGN AND DEVELOPMENT

When introducing the design and development of Egyptian fortifications one should keep in mind, that, in terms of engineering, the Nubian fortifications of the Middle Kingdom achieved a standard that cannot be

The method of construction of the protective wall at Aswan. The image shows two outer mud-brick walls which were then filled with granite rubble. (© A. Vogel)

Siege scene, the Tomb of Kheti, Beni Hassan No. 17. Among the famous wall paintings from the rock tombs at Beni Hassan are some exceptional scenes of siege warfare. Whether or not they illustrate the historical event of the storming of Herakleopolis, thus documenting the end of the First Intermediate Period, remains uncertain. The image supports the idea that the Egyptian architects favoured crenellated walls with wooden-supported bartizans. After P. E. Newberry.

found anywhere in Western Europe before the Early Modern period.

Our understanding of the architectural characteristics of Middle Kingdom fortresses has been mainly influenced by the unique abundance of archaeological remains belonging to the chain of fortresses situated between the first and the second cataracts. These fortifications have been thoroughly investigated by teams from various nations in the course of the UNESCO salvage campaign, which was launched in the 1960s following the construction of the Aswan High Dam in order to preserve the ancient Nubian heritage of the region.

It was common knowledge for more than 30 years that all mud-brick fortresses located between these cataracts had been submerged by the floods of the Aswan High Dam. Sensationally, Derek Welsby, a Sudan archaeologist from the British Museum, discovered that two of the higher fortifications – the island fortress of Uronarti and Shalfak, built on the western Nile bank – are still above the water surface and therefore accessible for renewed research. But for the time being the information introduced here is based on the results of the UNESCO salvage campaign and earlier missions.

Materials

Mud-brick

The Nubian fortifications were nearly always built in mud-brick (e.g. Buhen, $37 \times 18 \times 12$cm [15 x 7 x 5in.]) and subjected to uniform building principles. The rising walls of the fortifications were once completely covered with white plaster, which can be found at Buhen and elsewhere. This was the only way to protect the walls against the damage caused by wind and rain.

A dried mud-brick is quite easy to break by bending, which puts a tension force on one edge, but makes a good strong wall where all the forces are compressive. Pieces of straw, on the other hand, have a lot of strength when you try to stretch them but almost none when you crumple them up. But if you embed pieces of straw in a block of mud and let it dry hard, the resulting mud-brick resists both squeezing and tearing and makes an excellent building material. The mud-brick now has both good compressive strength and good

tensile strength. The Egyptian architects benefited from the acquisition of this knowledge and built up walls and buildings of considerable height.

The enormous width (up to 8m [26ft]) and height (up to 14m [46ft]) of the Nubian fortifications called for measures to disperse and dissipate the tremendous compressive force. The Egyptian architects' countermeasure was the insertion of layers of rush mats at regular intervals (most commonly after six or seven rows of bricks) and by the inclusion of wooden beams transverse to the course of the brickwork. These so-called wall anchors or crossbeams are well known in the present-day construction of dry-walls. In addition supporting abutments were erected against the wall at regular intervals to divert the force from it. The lower layers were further strengthened, mostly with pieces of granite, which served the same purpose while at the same time giving additional protection against sapping.

Stone

Whereas the majority of the fortifications within the time frame under discussion were made of mud-brick, there are a few examples of stone-built fortifications. Among them were the already-mentioned circular-shaped fortress at Ras Budran/Sinai, whose walls, up to 7m (23ft) wide, were built of limestone blocks. The material might originate from a series of nearby limestone hills, 4–6km (2–4 miles) to the north. Further evidence comes from a less fortified feature in the Eastern desert, almost 30km (19 miles) east of modern Aswan. Here, at the site of Wadi el-Hudi, a camp made of roughly hewn limestones was built to house the men involved in the amethyst mining projects.

Issues around the reconstruction of Nubian fortifications

When excavated, most Nubian fortifications had been preserved up to only about half of their original wall height. This leaves a lot of room for reconstruction attempts. There are a number of different approaches to take

Wall painting in the tomb of Inti. An early example of Egyptian siege warfare, a wall painting from the 5th Dynasty tomb of Inti in Deshashe, shows soldiers trying to breach the section of the wall where two bastions flank the entrance gate. This piece of evidence supports the idea that the gate was thought to be the weakest spot, and thus the main focus of attacks against fortresses. After N. Kanawati, A. McFarlane, *Deshaha: the Tombs of Inti, Shedu and Others*, Australian Centre for Egyptology Reports 5 (Sydney, 1993) pl. 26.

with regards to the reconstruction of the parapet. Researchers assume that nearly all Nubian fortifications had wall projections. These projections were thought to be bastions or towers, reaching up to the parapet where they provided a platform to be used by one or two archers.

This approach has been influenced by the publication results of the excavations at Buhen by Emery and his team, who were the first to suggest extensive reconstruction proposals for the main wall. Emery and succeeding researchers founded their theories on architectural examples, in particular temple and palace enclosures and illustrations showing Assyrian stone-built fortresses. However, the straight comparison of stone and mud-brick architecture would assume equal parameters, which don't exist either in terms of the materials used or their functionality.

Two kinds of monuments have been neglected which – in my opinion – are more suitable for the reconstruction of fortification walls:

1. Images of 1st Intermediate Period and Middle Kingdom fortifications in so-called assault scenes
They frequently indicate abutments by showing sloping faces at the bases of the walls visible on the sides of the frontally displayed construction. None of the representations show protrusions of the main wall, which – if we consider the common reconstructions of Nubian fortresses – must have been a frequent architectural feature.

Therefore, it appears likely to assume a large number of abutments for these fortifications in spite of tiny protrusions of the wall that would have been useless in terms of defence, since they provide no protection for the wall's base.

A crenellated wall with wooden-supported bartizans is documented in various assault scenes. The one shown on page 18 is in the tomb Beni Hassan No. 17. These had the advantage of saving on building materials while at the same time maintaining an effective defence for the wall's base.

2. African and Near Eastern mud buildings from the Middle Ages and modern times which have been preserved until today.
The use of abutments as structual elements is commonplace in traditional earth architecture and well known from examples like the famous Mopti Mosque in Mali.

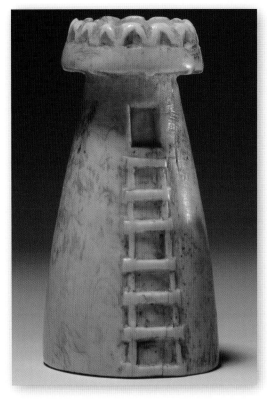

A game piece(?) depicting a watch tower, Egyptian Museum, Berlin 18031 (height 4.9cm). The model made of ivory comes from the early Dynastic royal cemetery at Abydos. The object sheds light on the appearance of real mud-brick watch towers, cone-shaped and crowned by a crenellated wood-supported platform that could have been in use as early as c.3100 BC. For safety reasons the entrance of those towers was moved to their upper floor, accessible via a pull-up ladder only.
(© Bildarchiv Preußischer Kulturbesitz, Berlin, 2009. Photo: Jürgen Liepe)

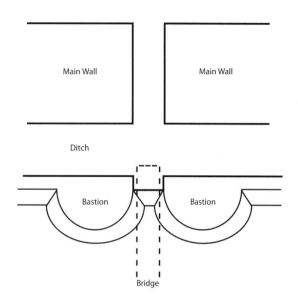

The main gate at the fortress of Kubban, Phase I. After W. B. Emery.

These regular wall protrusions don't need to be interpreted necessarily as towers. In my opinion the fighting platform provided by them would have been in most cases too small to give room for more than two archers. Powerless towers like this could not have been economically useful as they did not give much advantage to the defenders. On the contrary, they weakened the defensive front, since they created dead ground at the fortress's most sensitive spot: the base of the wall. Small bartizans, resting on wooden beams, however, provided additional flanking power for the defenders without the disadvantages of the small towers, and they are known from illustrations. Even Borchardt preferred the idea of balconies in his reconstruction of Semna-West. Therefore the regular small wall protrusions should be interpreted as abutments, which touched the wall at about two thirds of their height, with the purpose of dispersing the force resting upon the wall.

Defensive structures

The Nubian fortresses were subject to uniform building principles. Those situated on the Nile bank showed a rectangular layout. Their ramparts were surrounded by ditches of varying width and depth, which were protected by separate walls that ran parallel to the curtain. Those ditch-defences were further strengthened with horse-shoe-shaped bastions that projected into the ditch in the fashion of a modern caponier. Like these structures of modern-age fortifications, the ditch-defences weren't visible to an attacker unless he had reached the top of the glacis. Its double rows of loopholes would have produced a nasty surprise for any assailant that reached that far. A small wall on top of the glacis was the outermost element of these highly elaborate structures for staggered defence.

Gates

Gates are the most vulnerable feature within a fortification as they weaken the wall by creating an artificial gap. To overcome this problem, military architects of all ages and cultures have developed elaborate gateway solutions to ensure the protection of the entrance.

The Egyptian architects of Middle Kingdom Nubia developed complex entrance solutions to meet two requirements:

1) To allow easy access to the fortresses for their own people, material and pack mules and, at the same time.

2) To make the gate impregnable for a potential enemy.

These conflicting demands required compromises.

The inner west gate at Buhen. After W. B. Emery.

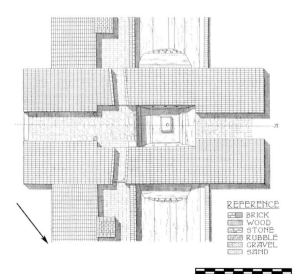

REFERENCE
- BRICK
- WOOD
- STONE
- RUBBLE
- GRAVEL
- SAND

0 1 2 3 4 5 6 7 8 9 10 m

One has to be seen in the approach from the desert: all main entrances to the Middle Kingdom Fortresses of the second building phase (reign of Senusret III) could be reached only through a very steep slope, and the floors of the gateway passages itself proceeded sloping up into the interior of the fort. Therefore, access to the fortress was difficult not only for any attacker, but also for the garrison itself. A common feature that is particularly observed in the Nubian context is the provision of flanking protection. This is the most common feature with main entrances in Middle Kingdom Nubia, as shown from examples such as Buhen, Mirgissa and many others.

In Middle Kingdom Nubia two main gate types are found, along with various sub-groups: huge and highly fortified gates facing the desert, served as the main entrance, as well as smaller and less fortified riverside gates that ensured access to reliable supplies of drinking water.

Main gates
The main entrance of a Nubian fortress was always potentially a weak spot within the defensive perimeter, but it sometimes developed into the strongest part of the fortification. The gatehouse designs can be compared in strength to the donjons of medieval castles. These were often strong enough to endure independently when everthing else had collapsed.

Usually these main gates were supported by a pair of large, flanking horseshoe-shaped bastions or rectangular towers protruding from the line of the curtain wall, while two smaller flanking towers often stretched into the inner ward. Examples like that of Mirgissa show even the road leading to the main entrance being kept under surveillance by a protective wall.

The protective wall at Aswan. The land route bypassing the unnavigable first cataract on the east bank of the Nile was protected by a massive mud-brick wall against potential attacks. The remains of this linear defence system have been preserved until today. The wall ran for *c*.7–8km (4–5 miles) from today's Fryal Garden area in the south of Aswan to the plain of Shellal. (© A. Vogel)

The gatehouse itself could also be supported by a number of other defences. Unfortunately, preservation of wall superstructures only up to half of their original height does not allow for convincing attempts at reconstruction. Any proposal regarding the reconstruction of the upper parts of gates has to be judged against this background.

Depending on the length of the gateway, a sequence of doors were incorporated in order to divide it up. For an effective protection against the impact of fire, a bronze cover for the wooden doors may well have been used, but none have been preserved as they would surely have been melted down for re-use.

Water gates
This type of gate can be observed in every single Nubian fortress. Its existence was essential, as it offered direct access to a stairway – at least partly covered – leading to the Nile. In terms of defence both water gate and covered river steps have to be seen as a single unit.

Postern gates
Postern gates are usually thought to have been built to simplify the amount of internal traffic, thus the existence or number of these gates within a fortress correlates to its size, as well as the presence of a ditch. While smaller fortresses like Uronarti, Shalfak and Askut, which were built on top of hills and do not have moats, omit this feature, their larger counterparts like Buhen possess them as a standard. The main reason for additional, smaller gates in an inner enclosure might be the need to offer direct access to the outer defence line.

B   RECONSTRUCTION OF THE FORTIFICATIONS AT BUHEN, LATE MIDDLE KINGDOM

Inscriptions prove that the mud-brick fortress of Buhen was in existence by year 5 of Senusret I. Now swallowed up by the waters of Lake Nasser, this view gives an idea of how the fortification might have looked. The reconstruction is based on the archaeological record of a major building stage dated to the late Middle Kingdom. By this time the outer defences had been strengthened tremendously by additional towers, a massive gateway and two new spur walls closing up to the Nile. Even if the appearance of the walls' upper parts remains unproven, iconographical evidence supports the idea of the solution provided here, in particular the protrusions interpreted as abutments, and the small balconies, resting on wooden beams.

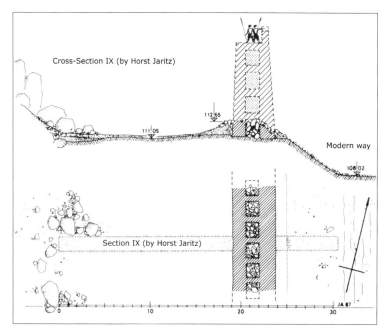

ABOVE LEFT

A reconstruction of the protective wall at Aswan. After H. Jaritz.

ABOVE RIGHT

The area around the first cataract. The map illustrates the defence system at Middle Kingdom Egypt's traditional southern border, combining archaeological and textual evidence. Sections of the fortifications on Elephantine Island and of the protective wall on the east bank are still visible, whereas further military installations still await discovery. Based on a map by H. Jaritz.

Ditches

For fortresses located on isolated bedrock an additional ditch was not considered to be an essential feature (e.g. at Askut, Shalfak, Uronarti). However, for fortifications situated on the Nile plain (e.g. Aniba, Kubban, Buhen) or other easily accessible locations, they are often found on the inland side of the fortifications.

Linear defences

We have archaeological hints that fortresses were linked by networks of walls that protected their hinterlands against possible attacks. One feature is known at modern Aswan and will be discussed in some detail.

In order to bypass the unnavigable first cataract, valuable goods from Nubia and the eastern desert – namely gold – were transported by land on the east bank of the Nile. An existing path between Konosso and the region across Elephantine can be traced back to the Old Kingdom. As caravans that used this path were a popular target for bands of marauders, it was decided at one point to construct a massive mud-brick wall in order to forestall these attacks.

Remains of this linear defensive system have been preserved until today and were examined for the first time in several small surveys during the 1980s conducted by Horst Jaritz.

Unfortunately, the date of this wall could not be confirmed for the Middle Kingdom so far – therefore it is questionable if it was part of the defence system during this period.

Today, the remains of the wall are still partially preserved with an average width of 5m (16ft) and a height up to 6m (20ft). On some spots the original height might have been about 10m (30ft). The wall was constructed with two faces of brickwork, supported by rush-mats after each seven to ten courses of bricks. Short cross-walls linked both faces and formed box-shaped sections, which were then filled with granite rubble. The wall ran from today's Fryal Garden's area in Aswan to the plain of Shellal. Even if the absolute dating of this structure is still of some doubt, it must be seen as an integral part of the

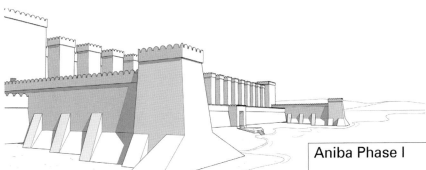

LEFT
The original appearance of the site of Aniba remains unknown. However, this reconstruction of the site at a later stage in its development gives us an idea of how it might have looked. (© F. Monnier)

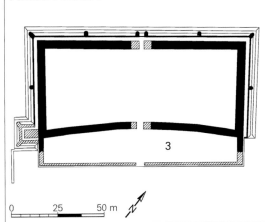

Aniba Phase I

3

0   25   50 m

defence system of the first cataract border region. In this function, the wall most likely served as a link between two fortifications: at its northern end a small fortification located opposite the southern end of Elephantine, and at its southern the fortress of Senmet, whose remains have not been discovered yet. The bypass was still in use during the time of the Roman occupation and safeguarded by several watchtowers on dominant heights in the foreland.

TOUR OF THE SITES: ANIBA, BUHEN, URONARTI, SEMNA-WEST

ABOVE
At Aniba the indigenous C-group population and the Egyptian occupying power lived close together. From the reign of Senusret I onwards, various building stages of a fortified Egyptian settlement can be traced.

Aniba

The fortress of Aniba (ancient name Miam) dates back to the early 12th Dynasty and thus is one of the oldest military installations known in Lower Nubia. Situated on the west bank of the Nile, 230km (143 miles) south of Aswan, the fortification was established in order to gain control over one of the most fertile plains of the Nubian Nile Valley. No less than seven building periods are attested at the site, which developed from a small fortified harbour installation (67 × 116m [220 x 381ft]) into a town of 8 hectares (20 acres).

The Egyptians were not the first to establish permanent settlements in the Aniba region. There is plenty of evidence that indigenous Nubians lived near the Nile here. Besides an earlier A-Group cemetery, there are also several C-Group settlements and cemeteries, the latter giving proof that the Nubians and the Egyptian occupyingpower lived close to each other.

Buhen

Of all Nubian fortifications Buhen (Bhn) can be considered the best known, both to scholars and the broader public. Intensively investigated first in the early 20th century and a second time in the course of the Nubian salvage campaign, a huge amount of information was revealed that allows us to describe its architecture and its history in some detail. Moreover, Buhen can be used here as a case study for a highly fortified harbour installation that underwent various alterations within its phases of ccupation between the early reign of Senusret I until its abandonment in the 20th Dynasty

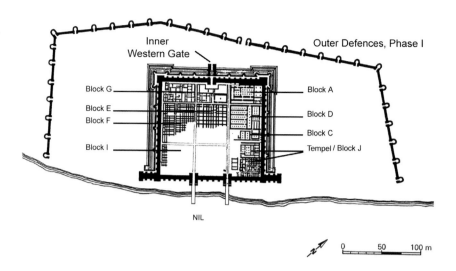

Buhen, Phase I showing the locations of the gates. After W. B. Emery.

Inner Western Gate

Outer Defences, Phase I

Block G

Block E
Block F

Block I

Block A

Block D

Block C

Tempel / Block J

NIL

0   50   100 m

(1951–1069 BC). The fortress belonged to a group of military installations that were built to the north of the second cataract on the flat or shelving banks of the Nile. Buhen was situated towards the southern end of this region on the west bank of the river, opposite the modern Nubian village of Degheim, 2km (1 mile) south of Wadi Halfa. Textual evidence demonstrates that the fort was in existence by year 5 of Senusret I (1951 BC).

Middle Kingdom, Phase I, outer defences
During the first phase, an outer enclosure made of mud-brick, 4m (13ft) thick, with 32 protruding bastions was built. The total length of the three desert-facing sides was 712m (2,335ft). The semicircular bastions, 2.15m (7ft) thick with a rubble core, projected 6.5m (21ft) from the wall's outer face at regular intervals of 22m (72ft). There is some evidence that access to the interior of the bastions was through 2m-wide (7ft) gates.

Only one entrance could be found in the outer enclosure wall, a gate, flanked by bastions 18 and 19 (counting from south to north). The feature was the first obstacle to be overcome when trying to reach the citadel.

Middle Kingdom, Phase II, outer defences
The final plan of the outer enclosure at Buhen, now up to 5.5m (18ft) thick, followed the course of its predecessor but possessed additional spur walls along the river front.

Two elaborate gates gave access to the Nile. Beneath the northern feature a stone-lined passage ensured a safe water supply in times of siege. Square features projected from the outer face of the wall spaced at more or less regular

---

C THE INNER WESTERN GATE AT BUHEN, MIDDLE KINGDOM

At Buhen a highly fortified tower-like gate positioned in the centre of the west wall served as the main entrance to the citadel. The reconstruction gives us an idea of Buhen's sophisticated defensive system: the gate and parts of the main wall, a narrow, brick-paved rampart with its own parapet wall, ditch and caponiers. While some scholars reconstruct the lower ramparts as a covered walkway, the author prefers the open solution as provided here.

That Buhen's archers were prepared to defend their fortress becomes clear by a double row of loopholes in the parapet wall. Although it has not been proven for the Middle Kingdom, but occurs on later gates, is the existence of propagandistic scenes (king smiting the enemies or presenting captured enemies before the god) on the outer faces of the gates' wings. The same goes for the existence of royal stelae at the gate's short sides.

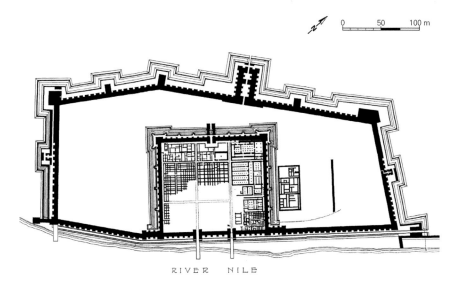

Buhen, Phase II. The altered ground plan shows a heavily stengthened set of defences, suggesting an overall improvement in the Egyptian siege warfare techniques. After W. B. Emery.

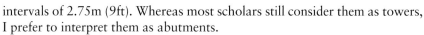

RIVER   NILE

Reconstruction of a section of the brick-paved rampart found at the foot of three sides of the main walls of Buhen. Whether it had a ceiling or not is unknown. The double rows of groups of three loopholes in the parapet wall, and three rows of triple loopholes in the bastions, were intended to allow for a crossfire by standing and kneeling archers. After Kemp, 2006, fig. 86.

intervals of 2.75m (9ft). Whereas most scholars still consider them as towers, I prefer to interpret them as abutments.

The foundations of five large towers protruding from the west wall have been discovered.

As a further obstacle a ditch, 6m (20ft) wide and 3m (10ft) deep, was cut in the rock running in front of the three inland sides. At one point, the ditch could be crossed via a rock-cut causeway to the north-west, which gave access to the main entrance of the outer defences.

The exact date of this monumental two-chamber-gate in the western wall is unknown, since it underwent different and complicated alterations. All we know is that it was built right on top of the first gate. It consisted of a great tower-like structure, measuring 47m (150ft) in length and 30m (100ft) in width, which possessed inner and outer buttresses. These projections are thought by many scholars to have been towers, reaching up to the parapet to provide a platform to be used by one or two archers. As pointed out above, I disagree with this reconstruction attempt.

Two additional gates, each 3m (10ft) wide are found in this second phase of fortification. It is difficult to determine if their use was restricted to offer access to the outer defence line solely for the garrison or if they might have been for incoming traffic as well. The gates were positioned in the centre of the north and south walls, consisting of a passageway 10m (30ft) long, stretching inwards and flanked by towers.

The citadel measured 150 × 138m (500 × 450ft), and was surrounded by a mud-brick wall of 5m (16ft) thickness. The original height of the walls might have been beteween 10 and 14m (33 and 46ft). In a similar manner to those traced on the outer defence walls, square features projected from the curtain at regular intervals. A lower brick-paved rampart with a fire-step behind its own parapet wall protected the base of the main wall. The parapet wall was pierced by a double row of loopholes,

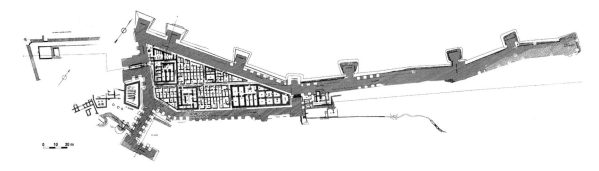

grouped in threes. At intervals semicircular bastions protruded into a ditch cut into the rock (7.3m [24ft] wide, and 3.1m [10ft] deep) that ran in front of the curtain wall.

Access to the citadel was restricted to a highly fortified, tower-like gate situated in the centre of the western side. Although its superstructure had been largely destroyed by later alterations, the Middle Kingdom foundations have been well enough preserved to give an idea of its general layout. The complex possessed a direct-access passage flanked by two rectangular towers aligned parallel to each other. The towers protruded inwards and outwards from the curtain wall. A wooden drawbridge that could be pulled back on rollers led across the dry ditch. The remains of this drawbridge were embedded in the side walls of the pit. It seems likely that the gate passage could be closed by sets of wooden doors at four spots along its length. A stone pivot socket could be traced in the outer face of the main wall.

Interior

As far as can be determined, the interior of the citadel of Buhen was occupied by rectangular brick buildings arranged around a rectilinear or orthogonal grid of streets. Unfortunately, the buildings in the south and east have been reduced to their foundation walls by destruction and erosion. So the regular cellular design – as shown in the excavator's plan – is misleading. By far the best-preserved building is the one in the citadel's north-west corner, most likely the commander's headquarters. A detailed description follows below.

The site of Buhen has been long used as an example of a fortress successfully stormed by the forces of Kush or Kerma. However, the assumption of Walter B. Emery that a massive destruction layer could have been caused through an assault by 'barbaric' Kerma Nubians at the end of the Middle Kingdom has been rebutted by S. T. Smith, who convincingly reinterpreted the records and brought forward the idea that they result from the violent reoccupation of the site by the 'civilized' Egyptians in the late 17th/early 18th Dynasty.

Uronarti

The fortress Khesef Iuntiu, 'repelling the Nubian troglodytes/tribesmen', was built on a hill 67m (220ft) above the low level of the Nile on the northern end of the island of Uronarti, 5km (3 miles) north of the frontier at Semna-West/Kumma/Semna-South. It formed part of the chain of fortresses in the second cataract region built by Senusret III

Ground plan of Uronarti. The reign of Senusret III (1882–1842 BC) saw Egyptian military architecture reach its first peak. New solutions were developed to make the best possible use of space. The ground plan of the island fortress of Uronarti illustrates the solutions found by military architects for the pressing issues of cramming accommodation into a limited amount of space.

Boundary stela from Uronarti on display in the National Museum Khartoum (SNM 451). The item dates from the sixteenth year of Senusret III and belongs to a group of stelae erected to define Egypt's southern border.

The island fortress of Uronarti. A couple of years ago the Sudan archaeologist Derek Welsby announced an outstanding discovery. Even well-informed scholars had believed for more than 30 years that all mud-brick fortresses located between the first and second cataracts had been submerged by the floods caused by the Aswan Dam. Sensationally, Welsby revealed that two of the higher placed fortifications, the island fortress of Uronarti (seen here) and Shalfak, built on the western bank of the Nile, remained above the surface of the water. (© P. Wolf)

in order to defend his newly established southern border. However, we know of various campaigns within the king's reign undertaken in areas lying further to the south.

As mentioned earlier, the fortress of Uronarti surprisingly survived the flooding of Lake Nasser.

A stela found overthrown at the edge of the temple bastion, thus outside the walls and now on display in the National Museum of Khartoum (SNM 451), tells us about Uronarti's construction, or at least its inauguration. The text, an almost exact copy of those of the more famous Semna stela (Berlin 1157) quoted above, differs in precisely those lines that refers to the building of a fortress. The text of the Uronarti stela reads: 'Stela made in the year 16, third month of Peret (= winter time), when the fortress "Repelling the Iuntiu" was built', whereas the corresponding text on the Semna stela refers to Egypt's border at Hech: 'Year 16, month 3 of Peret: His majesty made the southern boundary at Hech (region of Semna.)'

Defences
The fortress was triangular in shape (57 × 114 × 126m [190 × 380 × 413ft]) in order to fit on the rocky outcrop upon which it was built. A massive spur wall with protruding bastions in intervals on its western outer face extended 250m (820ft) towards the north. The remains of the mud-brick curtain wall, up to 8m (26ft) thick with the usual layer of reed mats, suggests an original height of up to 14m (45ft). The common rectangular abutments at regular intervals can also be found here.

Access to the fortress was restricted to one main gate. This was approached from the south and went up a steep slope, while flanking walls protruded southwards from the main wall, thus protecting the gate. They

D   THE ISLAND FORTRESS OF URONARTI, MIDDLE KINGDOM

The fortress of Uronarti is one of two sites that survived the flooding of Lake Nasser. Still standing above the surface of the water in the region of the second cataract, the fortification consists of a large triangular enclosure with a massive wing wall extending towards the north-east crest of the island. Its height above the low level of the Nile is 67m (220ft). The fortress was built or at least inaugurated by Senusret III of the 12th Dynasty,

as proved by an important stela dated to his 16th year found at the site.

This reconstruction gives us an idea of Uronarti as it would have appeared in the late 12th Dynasty. We see the main entrance additionally protected by lower walls at the left and the secondary entrance including the river steps and the spur wall at the right.

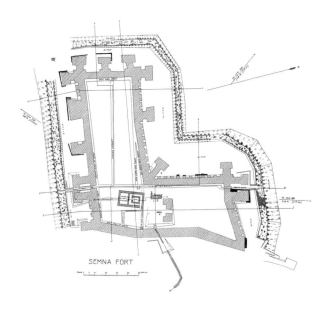

SEMNA FORT

Ground plan of Semna West. The fortress of Semna-West was founded under Senusret III. Its unique L-shape was chosen by the architect in order to meet the topographical situation. After D. Dunham and J. M. A. Janssen.

Remains of the fortress of Semna-West. The L-shaped fortress of Semna-West belongs to a sequence of three fortifications that guarded the southern end of the second cataract. An impressive dry ditch protected the feature at its three inland-facing sides. L. Borchardt, *Altägyptische Festungen an der zweiten Nilschnelle* Wiesbaden, 1923, pl. 1b.

were 6m (20ft) wide and ended with strong towers (total length including thickness of the curtain: 23m [75ft]). Buttresses were placed on their outer faces. At least three wooden sills were found, indicating that the doors were situated 5m (16ft) from the south end of the passage, as well as 4 and 2m (13 and 4ft) from the inner end. The passage between the outer and middle doors was lined by a mud-brick wall (0.8m [3ft] thick), narrowing the passage from 2.7 to 2.3m (9 to 8ft).

River stair

The northern gate was built as the familiar passage leading through the northern wall. The passage was 8m (26ft) long and 2.6m (9ft) wide. The remains of their wooden sills shows the location of two doors, 4m (13ft) apart from each other. The floor of the passageway was originally paved with stone slabs, and a water drain passed through the gate. It turned east down the sloping approach to the river stair, which ran 250m (820ft) to the north before reaching the Nile.

The northern gate not only gave access to the Nile steps, but also to a temple area. A northern wing, strengthened by buttresses, gave additional shelter and ran for a distance of 250m (820ft) beyond the gate.

Interior

The inner layout of Uronarti shows a highly effective space-saving concept. Its example proves that the Egyptian master architects did a great job in ancient Nubia by putting up distinct buildings within a confined space. The way that they incorporated features like barracks, headquarters, granaries, magazines and workshops into their military installations indicates a masterplan that could be adjusted to the topographical situation when required.

Like elsewhere, the soldiers at Uronarti had to live in cramped conditions, here in the common tripartite barracks, whereas the commander profited from his high rank by living and working in spacey accommodation with all the amenities.

Three complexes served as barracks, designated by the excavators as block I, block VIII, and block X. The walls of the barrack blocks were 50cm (20in.)

thick. Each building consisted of an anteroom of 4.5 × 2.5m (15 × 8ft), and two inner rooms of 5 × 2m (16 × 7ft). How these barracks might have looked and what the soldier's life might have been like will be described further below.

Semna-West

During the reign of Senusret III three fortifications protected the southernmost part of the region of the second cataract: Semna-South, Semna-West and Kumma. Located around the narrowest gorge in the entire course of the Nile, two of them were situated on the western bank: Semna-South and Semna-West (the distance between them was 1.5km [1 mile]), a further one, Kumma, stood opposite Semna-West on the east bank. Between Semna-South and Semna-West a mud-brick wall seems to have existed in order to fence off the region to the west. The remains of such a feature, 2m (6ft) wide and resting on a stone foundation, can be traced at both sites.

The earliest evidence for an Egyptian presence at Semna-West – the site to be examined most closely – dates back to year 8 of Senusret III. The so-called smaller boundary stela (Berlin 14753) demonstrates Egypt's strong interest in trade relations with its southern 'enemies' and reveals the Pharaoh's intent to control the border totally. This remarkable text prevents – at least in theory! – any Nubian from crossing the border except in order to trade at Mirgissa, a fortress situated approximately 40km (25 miles) to the north:

The smaller stela from Semna-West. The object dates from Senusret's III eighth regnal year. Its text offers an insight in the Egyptian Nubian policy in the 12th dynasty. After C. Loeben.

> Southern boundary, made in the year 8, under the Majesty of the King of Upper and Lower Egypt, Khakaukare (Senusret III), who is given life forever and ever: in order to prevent any Nubian from crossing it when going north, neither on land nor by ship as well as any herds of the Nubians, except a Nubian who shall come to trade in Iqen (Mirgissa) or as a messenger. Every good thing shall be done with them, but without allowing a ship of the Nubians to pass by Heh (Semna region), going downstream forever.

Another boundary stela from Senusret's 16th regnal year (Berlin 1157), already quoted above, can also be connected with the building or inauguration of the fortress.

The fortification was L-shaped and situated on a promontory on the west bank of the Nile. Granite rubble was used to even out the building site. If anybody approached the fortress from the south or the north he saw at first a glacis about 6m (20ft) wide, and an outer wall about 7.5m (25ft) wide, plus a ditch of varying widths cut into the rock, and finally the massive main wall.

E   **NEXT PAGE: EGYPT'S SOUTHERN FRONTIER AT THE SECOND CATARACT AS OF THE LATE 12TH DYNASTY**

The fortress system at Semna consisted of three installations that not only provided military protection, but also regulated trade and diplomatic traffic to the north. The southernmost fortress was Semna-South. From here a mud-brick wall, fencing off the territory to the west, led to the huge fortress of Semna-West, situated 1.5km (1 mile) to the north. Unique owing to its L-shape, the fortification can be considered as the most important within this region. A further fortress, Kumma, stood opposite to Semna-West on the east bank of the Nile. A huge amount of rock inscriptions traced in the neighbourhood of the fortifications records the monitoring system of the garrisons as well as the precise measuring of the Nile level.

The ramparts of the fortress were 5–8m (16–26ft) wide and built in mud-bricks (32 × 14 × 8cm [13 × 6 ×3in.]); after each five courses of bricks a layer of reed mats and wooden beams was laid. The interior space of the fortress was 7,865.5 square metres (84,663 square feet), along with an additional west wing (42.1 × 89.5m [138 × 300ft]) and north wing (37 × 110.5m [120 × 360ft]). The assumed height of the main wall might have been up to 14m (45ft).

Regular access to the fortress was restricted to two main gates, which were connected by a street plastered with granite running south–north. Both gates, 15 and 16m (50 and 52ft) long, are of the same type: a huge one-chamber gate protruding from the perimeter wall. At these spots the ditch was filled with rubble to form a crossing, and, at least in the south, a drain placed underneath. Both gates had two wooden doors and it seems likely that the space between the doors was accessible from the rampart above, so that any intruder who broke through the outer door would be exposed within a narrow enclosure to projectiles from above.

As already stated, the water supply of the Nubian forts was of the utmost importance, especially in times of siege, and Semna-West was no exception. Within its eastern wall a door opened to a set river steps leading to the Nile. The feature was protected in its upper part by a substantial dry-stone masonry wall.

Interior
Within this unique L-shaped fortress the western wing was largely reserved for barracks. The area north and south of the so-called Cross Street provided space for two long double rows of the common tripartite building type, built back to back. The single units measured 8 × 5m (26 × 16ft), the individual rooms being 5 × 2m (16 × 7ft).

As the main area of the northern part has not been excavated, its original use remains uncertain. However, beneath the New Kingdom temple, which was dedicated to the deified Senusret III and the Nubian god Dedun, the remains of a Middle Kingdom temple have been found. Some further evidence supports the assumption of a second Middle Kingdom temple in the south-west corner of the western wing. Here traces of a 20 × 25m (65 × 82ft) building have been found.

THE LIVING SITES

What was it like to live at the border of the Egyptian Empire? Did it imply boredom or stress? What do we know about the soldier's living conditions? What kind of daily activities did he have to do? What did he eat? How was he remunerated? Did a transfer to a Nubian fortress imply a setback in his military career or might it be seen as a professional promotion? What spectrum of professions is recorded in these fortresses? Is it possible to reconstruct an ideal garrison? What information might be traced from the documents in order to highlight the administrative machinery as well as the military service? Do we have any information about the relationship between the garrison and the locals? Are there any hints for combats in the vicinity of a fortress? These and many other questions will be raised to illustrate the living conditions of a soldier working in an Egyptian fortification in Nubia.

The barracks

The question where and how to accommodate the garrison was one of the main issues to deal with when planning a fortress. To house a huge number of soldiers in a very confined space requires a number of space-saving solutions. Uniform barracks provided the solution for this dilemma and can be found in many cultures.

The tomb of Mahu, the chief of police at Amarna, contains many unusual scenes. Among them is this unique representation of a three-storey watch-tower that gives us an idea how the interior of these and earlier towers might have looked like. After A. Badawy.

The Egyptians were no exception. They built rectangular houses of 32–44 square metres (344–474 square feet), consisting of three rooms. One cross-rectangular room opened into two elongated ones, most likely the soldiers' resting and sleeping rooms. The anteroom might have served as an place to prepare food, for dining, storage and for the maintenance of weapons and equipment. Due to their uniform architectural pattern and – of course – their presence in large numbers, barracks can be identified in several well-preserved fortresses like Serra-East, Mirgissa, Shalfak, Askut, Uronarti and Semna-West.

The example shown on page 40 illustrates their principles:
A rectangular ground floorplan consisting of three rooms with an entrance facing the street, most often grouped in two rows of houses with sharing back walls. One can compare the form and function of these houses with those known from the two workmen's villages at Qasr el-Saga, which served the basalt quarries of the Gebel Katrani in the Northern Fayum. In Qasr el-Saga each house consists of a cross-rectangular entrance room opening to five elongated, neighbouring rooms. The excavators found archaeological evidence that the anteroom served as a cooking and dining area, a function that the anteroom in the Nubian fortresses might share as well.

A soldier's wooden bread-ration token from the fortress of Uronarti. Eleven plastered items representing various loaves of bread were found in a storeroom within the fortress, all but one bearing an incised inscription, difficult to translate. The round flat loaf with raised centre shown here refers to 70 loaves of bread. The item is pierced, obviously for a loop to hang it from. 12th Dynasty, year 33 of Amenemhat III, Museum of Fine Arts, Boston (Inv-No 24.732), Harvard University–Boston Museum of Fine Art Expedition, (Photograph © 2010 Museum of Fine Arts, Boston)

Commander's residence or headquarters

One of the most remarkable constructions inside a Nubian fortress was the commander's residence or headquarters. This structure is notable due to its comparatively large size and attractive housing conditions. However, its identification with specific architectural remains within the Nubian fortresses is not that simple and has led to different theories bring put forward by the excavators. First of all, one has to bear in mind that we do not know if the ancient Egyptians made a distinction between headquarters and residence like the Romans did between *principia* and *praetorium*.

Regardless of the social status of the commander, it seems quite obvious from the Egyptian ideas of rigid hierarchy that he did not share a lodgings with his soldiers. In Roman forts the centurion lived in the larger officer's room at the end of the soldiers' barrack block.

F   **A REPRESENTATIVE MILITARY BARRACK IN A NUBIAN FORTRESS, MIDDLE KINGDOM**

Low-ranking Egyptian soldiers had to live in uniform barracks, which were found in almost every single fortress. The conventional room arrangement consisted of three rooms, covering a space of 32–44 square metres (344–474 square feet). One cross-rectangular anteroom – to be thought of as a court – opened to two elongated inner rooms. As the archaeological record does not allow a final statement as to whether those buildings possessed one or two storeys, both solutions are offered here side by side.

The first solution favours a building with one floor and an accessible roof, whereas the second solution prefers a building with two floors and an accessible roof.

There is some evidence that the court served as an interactive place to prepare food, for dining, storage and for the maintenance of weapons and equipment. The two inner rooms (of the first and an assumed second floor) should most likely be identified as the soldiers' resting and sleeping rooms.

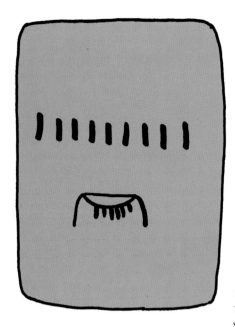

Gold weight from Uronarti. Finds of gold weights within Nubian fortresses testify to their importance as sites for the collection, storing and transferring of valuables. (© V.-R. Bach-Berkhahn)

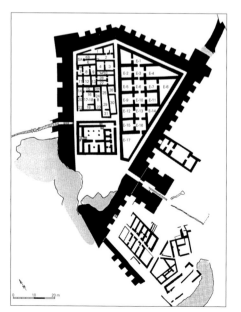

Fortress of Askut. This ground plan sheds light on the importance of food supply with almost half the interior space devoted to granaries (E). After S. T. Smith.

Against this background some principles should be taken into account when trying to identify the commander's residence:

The building should be significantly larger than a barrack.
It should be prestigious and imposing.
It might have an upper floor.
It should be the only one of its kind within the fortress.
It should provide direct access to the ramparts.
It should be positioned at a strategic place.

At Buhen, all these requirements are met by the so-called Block A.

A building of *c.*1,000 square metres (10,800 square feet) situated in the north-west corner of the inner fortress most likely served as the garrison's headquarters/commander's residence. It was built against the main wall to which a staircase offered direct access. The house possessed at least two floors, as we know from the remains of a second staircase. Both stairs could be easily reached from the building's main entrance via a series of two one-pillared halls. In the centre, various smaller rooms were grouped around three-pillared halls.

It seems clear that the high-ranking officers in an Egyptian fortress would not miss out on any comforts while working and living far away from their homeland. The comfort of their homes, even in cramped conditions, might be explained by one of their most sensitive tasks: the control of the cross-country trade in gold and its handling within the fortress. An Egyptian Pharaoh would never have accepted any irregularities, but – being aware that his officers were outside the range – some luxuries for them might have be seen as a way to counteract corruption.

Treasuries

Where might valuables like gold have been stored in a Nubian fortress? Most likely in a treasury, a building that has been found in various sites. The ancient Egyptian term for treasury was *pr-ḥd*, meaning 'house of silver'. One hundred and thirteen mud-seal impressions from Uronarti name its treasury (*pr-ḥd mnn.w Ḥsf'Iwn.tj.w*). Most of them were found in a specific building next to the granary. This block has a cross-rectangular courtyard leading to three narrow, parallel-elongated rooms. Apart from the treasury of Uronarti we have textual evidence of a *pr-ḥd* at Askut, Semna-South and Mirgissa. Unfortunately, their archaeological identification has not been possible so far.

Granaries

Storage facilities for grain were an important part of the internal layout of a fortress. One hundred and sixty mud-seal impressions mention the granary at Uronarti (*šnw.t mnn.w Ḥsf'Iwn.tj.w* = granary of the fortress of Uronarti). These reveal internal administrative processes, documenting the filling or emptying of the granary, as every time this procedure was executed the seals at the granary doors had to be broken and re-sealed.

Large granaries were able to provide food for the soldiers garrisoned in the fortress. Moreover, examples like Askut have shown that the Nubian fortresses must have served as supply bases for an army on campaign as well. The granary at Askut occupies so much of the interior space that this entire site can be considered a fortified grain store.

The Nubian fortresses contain the uniform Middle Kingdom granary type that is quite easy to identify: nearly square rooms with connecting doorways formed into separate blocks. These granaries were, most likely, filled and emptied from above. The roofs of the individual silos might have been vaulted, as sometimes shown in contemporary models and paintings.

However, Josef Wegner, who excavated a 10-chamber granary complex in the town of Wach-Sut at Abydos, argued they they might have been simply open at the top with access via ladders.

An example of a small model from the tomb of Meketre

helps to understand the procedures executed in a granary. At the anteroom, the arriving wheat or barley is carefully measured in the presence of several accountants. They are checking what might have been tax lists and making tallies. The anteroom gives access to another chamber. Its entrance is controlled by the familiar figure of the granary overseer, who is keeping a sharp eye on everybody who enters or leaves the building. From the second anteroom the grain is carried in baskets up a flight of stairs and dumped into three large bins.

Shell bearing the cartouche of Senusret I. Scallop shells like the one here are well known from the early 12th Dynasty. Thought to be symbols of honour they were given by the Pharaoh to his most deserving soldiers. They usually possess two drilled holes so that they could be attached to fix a loop. (© V.-R. Bach-Berkhahn)

A market stall at Khan el-Khalili, Cairo's most prominent souk. Through to the present day bread and fresh vegetables have been the pillars of traditional Egyptian cuisine, which allows for a comparison of the dietary habits across time. (© Christine Wolf)

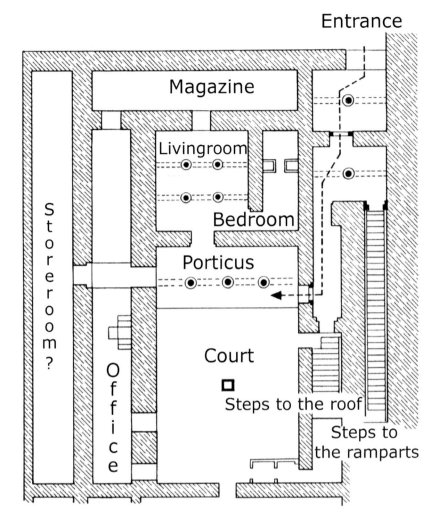

Entrance

Magazine

Livingroom

Bedroom

S t o r e r o o m ?

O f f i c e

Porticus

Court

▫ Steps to the roof

Steps to the ramparts

In Buhen, Block A in the north-west corner of the inner fortress most likely served as the garrison's headquarters. It was built against the main wall to which a staircase offered direct access. The house had at least two floors, which we know from the remains of a second staircase. Both stairs could easily be reached from the building's main entrance via a series of two one-pillared halls. In the centre, various smaller rooms were grouped around three-pillared halls. After D. Arnold.

Magazines (wḏ3)

From textual evidence the existence of another building type, the so-called (wḏ3) magazine, is well documented in Nubian fortresses. We know them from Semna-South, Shalfak, Askut and Mirgissa.

However, the archaeological data here is even more difficult to interpret. A complex of buildings in the north-western corner of the inner fortress of Mirgissa served – at least in the 13th Dynasty at the latest – as an arsenal and workshop for weapons. But these three rooms are not necessarily a wḏ3, especially as there is another, specific term for arsenal: pr-ꜥḥ3.w 'house of weapons'. Hundreds of flint tips for spears and arrows, bows, wooden handles and skins for shields have been found in these rooms.

G   RECONSTRUCTION OF THE HEADQUARTERS AT BUHEN, MIDDLE KINGDOM

A huge building located in the north-west corner of the citadel most likely served as the garrison's headquarters/commander's residence. Its strategic position is evident from the fact that it was built against the main wall to which a staircase offered direct access. Thus, the commander could easily access the ramparts if required.

The house had at least two storeys, as we can trace from the remains of a second staircase. Both stairs could be reached from the building's main entrance via two one-pillared halls. This reconstruction shows an official reception in the audience hall. A guard at the entrance checks to see if the visitors are authorized to enter.

The ditch and ramparts of the Middle Kingdom fortress of Kubban. After Emery-Kirwan, p. 135, plate 4, above, left.

Eating habits

The diet of an Egyptian garrison in Nubia was not only restricted to the bread and beer produced from the grain stored in the huge granaries.

A rich deposit of several fruits has been found at the island fortress of Askut. The wide range of different species found includes sycamore fig, dom (a type of palm), dates and many others. Net-weights and hooks, recovered from several fortresses, prove that fresh fish was also on the menu. This does not come as a suprise given that all fortresses were situated close to the Nile.

However, the main diet for the garrison remained bread and beer, and a number of varieties could be made from both barley and wheat.

The raw ingredients stored in the huge granaries could be broken down into smaller quantities as required. An amazing group of 11 bread-shaped wooden objects discovered in room number F5 at Uronarti should also be mentioned in this context.

Despite the fact, that their inscriptions are extremly difficult to understand, they are generally thought to be military tokens. The texts on them concern deliveries of provisions for the Egyptian troops stationed in the fortress of Uronarti.

Two different mathematical values are introduced at the same time: *tssrt* and *psw*.

Recent mathematical studies have defined the *psw* value as the number of loaves of bread or jars of beer that one might get out of a *heqat* (4.8 litres) of grain.

A soldier's haircut, tomb of Userhet, TT 56.

Garrison numbers

The question of how many soldiers might have lived in a Nubian fortress has often been raised. In the case of the famous Middle Kingdom fortress of Buhen, Emery favoured the method of looking at the total length of the lower and upper ramparts and assuming that each embrasure had to be protected by one archer. He ended up with a defending force of 804 men and added a further 25 per cent for officers and support troops, thus coming up with a total number for the inner fortress of 1,005. Another method thought up by Barry Kemp, is to look for the capacities of the granaries within the fortresses.

Kemp, who was the first to study the large Middle Kingdom granaries in great detail, attempted to calculate the capacity of each individual granary. He simultaneously warned about the limiting factors of such calculations, as we are in the dark whether one can take the original height of the Mirgissa granary – 3.4m (11ft) – as a standard height for all other buildings. Furthermore, the question of its possible filling height also needs to be considered (Kemp assumed 2.8m [9ft]), as well as the filling intervals. It is also unsure whether animals had to be feed, and if the silos were reserved for grain only. Other options could include lentils and other pulses. The ongoing analysis of botanical and flotation samples from the granary in Abydos might clear this question up.

Finally, one also has to bear in mind that grain was needed for the production of both bread and beer. This fact makes an exact calculation more complicated, since we do not know their relation to each other.

As one might imagine, both models have weak spots and in my opinion a third approach is more promising. Assuming that one is dealing with a well-preserved fortress, a figure for the garrison could be obtained by adding up the total number of barracks and multiplying this by the presumed number of soldiers living in each unit. Even this approach must be used with care since the numbers of floors within a barracks are not known for sure. Felix Arnold recently discussed this in relation to the balance of sand to mud within mud-bricks. He pointed out that smaller mud-brick walls might have supported a second floor if they contained a huge amount of sand, which stabilizes the construction. The old assumption that only wide/thick walls could have supported additional floor levels is therefore no longer tenable.

Rock inscription from Semna-West, No. 509. A large number of rock inscriptions in the neighbourhood of the Nubian fortresses refer to soldiers garrisoned there. They sometimes contain important hints about their titles and duties. The example given here was found at Semna-West and dates to the early 13th Dynasty. It belongs to a couple of blocks rescued from the floods of Lake Nasser and moved to the garden of the National Museum in Khartoum. The four lines read:
Nile level of year 3,
Under the king of Upper and Lower Egypt, 'Imenemhat-Sobekhetep',
when the royal seal-bearer, the general Ren-Seneb
was in command of the fortress of 'Semna-West'. (© Miriam Lahitte)

The soldier's haircut

A flint blade, a copper razor with a recurving handle and abundant lumps of black curly hair indicated room no. 10 at Askut as the barber's quarters.

Hairdressers are well recorded in ancient Egypt. In the Old Kingdom their title is *jrj schen*, meaning, 'to make the hair', thus fitting the main task of their job very well. However, it seems most likely that besides cutting the hair and shaving their customers' beards, delousing might also have been part of their service. This could be what is illustrated in an amazing genre scene from the tomb of the scribe Userhet in Thebes (TT 56), dating from the reign of Amenhotep II. This scene shows a large number of recruits waiting to be attended to by two men. The common explanation that those soldiers are going to receive their obligatory new military hair cut, remains unproven since the barbers do not seem to have any working tools. Nevertheless, the ancient equivalent of the 'short back and sides' given to recruits into the army today might well have formed an essential part of the process of removing any trace of individuality in the ancient Egyptian army as well.

The higher the *psw* value, the less grain the bread or beer would contain, through the relative grain is not mentioned.

The *trsst* value is derived from the 12th Dynasty Papyrus Reisner I, where an exact number is given of how many *tssrt* rations a group of persons is allowed to receive. The text mentions 20 different persons who receive eight *tssrt* rations a day. The *psw* values given in the Uronarti tallies varies from 60 to 80.

One of the tokens kept in the Museum of Fine Arts in Boston contains a dated inscription on its concave face: 'Year 33 under the majesty of the good god Ni-maat-Ra (=Amenemhat III), living forever: memorial (?)of the time of cooking 70.'

Below the inscription is a Djed-sign (indicating eternity, thus duration) in black ink. They could be fastened to another object by means of wooden tenons inserted through a series of holes.

Model granary from tomb of Meketre. Middle Kingdom, c.1981–1975 BC. Wood, plaster, paint, linen, grain, height 36.5cm (14 ³/₈ in.), length 74cm (29 ¹/₈ in.), width 58cm (22 ¹³/₁₆ in). Egyptian; Thebes, Meketre. Rogers Fund and Edward S. Harkness Gift, 1920. (Image copyright © The Metropolitan Museum of Art/Art Resource, NY)

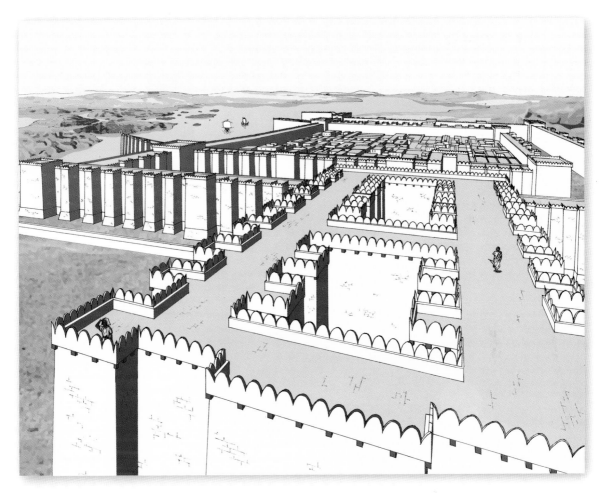

Regardless of how much grain or how many loaves of bread a single soldier might have received, he will have undoubtedly suffered from worn teeth, a problem faced by every ancient Egyptian from Pharaoh to worker. The bread contained a high level of grit, introduced either into the flour as it was milled or as wind-blown sand and dust. Over a period of time, this wore down the enamel of the teeth, causing as best some discomfort and pain, and, at worst, serious abcesses and infections, which could be fatal.

With respect to the soldier's diet, water supply was vital, especially during times of siege. Therefore, highly fortified river gates and water steps were built to guarantee its permanent availability. As already mentioned above, these essential features are found in every single fortress in Nubia.

Mirgissa, the outer northern gate. The fortress of Mirgissa, situated on the western bank of the Nile, c.16km (10 miles) south of Buhen, is renowned for its impressive outer northern gate. Military architects were well aware that, as the weakest spot within the defence, the gate area had to be highly fortified in order to withstand possible attacks. (© F. Monnier)

Hygiene

The issue of the possible location of sanitary installations within Egyptian fortresses has never been discussed. However, it seems clear, that they didn't invent a solution like the Romans did when they established their highly economic latrines.

The only hint one can find within the literature on Middle Kingdom fortresses is the identification of room no. 12 in the headquarters of Buhen. Situated directly under the stairway leading to the second floor, its interpretation as a toilet seems mainly influenced by this location, this being well known from contemporary house types. However, there might have been

The New Kingdom Temple of Khnum from Kumma, National Museum Khartoum.

toilets in more representative houses like headquarters. For the garrison itself, the Egyptian architects would not have wasted space for permanent toilet-rooms. The soldiers might have used the common sand-filled cups, possibly in combination with wooden toilet-chairs. We will never know if they developed a feature like the medieval (and early modern) rampart-toilet, since none of the walls of the Nubian fortresses have been preserved up to their original height.

Temples and private cult

During the New Kingdom period many temples were built within the Nubian fortresses dedicated to Egyptian and local gods, such as the temple of Khnum at Kumma. It has been assumed that they might have replaced Middle Kingdom predecessors in a continuity of the cult. Unfortunately, this assessment is not based on stratified building sequences.

Some of the architectural structures which have been thought to be temples should actually be identified as headquarters. However, there is some evidence, that sanctuaries were only integrated within a fortress – especially during the critical 12th Dynasty – if ample space was available within the walls. Where space was limited, as in Uronarti, the places for ritual worship were mainly located outside the fortified enclosure. The state cult might have been performed either by professional priests, or by officials as a part of their routine duties.

However, the archaeological records indicate that we should not underestimate the private cult of individual soldiers. The numerous finds of ritual figurines show that there was a considerable amount of personal religious practice performed by the garrison.

The official cult was directed towards the state gods like Horus and Hathor, as well as local gods such as Satet, Anukis, Khnum or Dedun. At

Askut, for instance, expressions of private religious practice were multi-faceted and changing. In the Middle Kingdom period the emphasis was placed much more on the veneration of ancestors and perhaps household deities like Bes and Taweret.

A large number of clay figures have been found in Nubian fortresses. Some scholars think of these as ritual objects while others contend that they are toys. Since the archaeological context does not offer any help in most cases, we remain in the dark about their original function.

There is one exception to this lack of knowledge, and that comes with the so-called execration figures. Politics was also an affair of magic in Egypt during this period. The Pharaoh did not only count on his armies in order to repel attackers or on his diplomats to circumvent hostile nations; he also counted on his magicians to bewitch enemy leaders. The southern frontier defence programme of the Middle Kingdom included priest-magicians whose role was to weaken by sorcery the southern rulers whose invasions terrorized the Egyptians. The enemy leader is shown as a prisoner, and an identifying text completes the magic mechanism: 'the Prince of X, son of A and B, and all those defeated with him'. The names and titles of the bewitched person are also inscribed on the clay vases that were then broken in order to bring about the victim's ruin. Figurines like this have been found at digs in Mirgissa and other sites in Nubia. These same magic techniques were also used against Asian rulers on the northern frontier.

Two execration figures from Mirgissa. The Egyptian understanding of warfare included various magical practices in order to defeat the enemy. Thus, it does not come as a surprise that even in the environment of Nubian fortresses deposits of execration figures were found. Usually made of clay the captives are showed kneeling, and bound. They bear Hieratic inscriptions naming the enemies to be cursed. It can be assumed that the figures were buried after a ceremony in which the potential enemies were named in the presence of official witnesses. Our two examples come from a deposit found at Mirgissa, dated to the 12th Dynasty. (© V.-R. Bach-Berkhahn)

The north gate of Mirgissa also provides some evidence of leisure time activities pursued by the garrison. This gate is one of the most impressive gates found in ancient Nubia. It bears comparison with the far better-known gates of the outer and inner defences at Buhen. It is in this highly fortified structure that the excavators discovered a game of Senet, an ancient Egyptian board game, carved into the paving. This illustrates that the guards on duty might have been bored sometimes.

Another game that seems to have been pretty popular with the soldiers is the 'Jackals and Hounds' game. Several fragments of game boards modeled out of clay have been found in Nubian fortresses. The rules of this game are not known, but it appears to be a race between a team of five jackals and a team of five hounds (originally peg playing pieces) around a palm tree to be inserted in the big hole on each board.

The make-up of the garrison

The epigraphic sources reveal more than 100 different professions in the Middle Kingdom. Unfortunately, we are unable to break these titles down to reconstruct the composition of an ideal garrison within a shorter period of time, like the reign of one single king. However, it is nevertheless of some interest to assign the recorded titles to various groups.

First of all we have to mention the military. The attested titles range from the highest-ranking officers down to simple privates like bowmen (*jrj-pd.t*). We are informed, for instance, about a *jmj-r3 mšˁ-wr* (general of the generals = highest military rank) Renseneb, who commanded the fortress of Semna-West under Amenemhat-Sebekhetep II in the 13th Dynasty (1785–1650 BC). Interestingly, up to the early 13th Dynasty, all known commanders bear different titles. The well-known title of *tzw*, usually assigned to a commander of a fortress in the New Kingdom, occurs several times but seems not mandatory.

What might have qualified an officer to command a smaller or a larger fortress? Most likely the size of the troop he had led on earlier occasions. This idea is supported by the title of an officer who was holding the rank of a *šms.w nj hq3* while commanding the fortress of Askut during the reign of the king Amenemhat-Senebef in the 13th Dynasty. We know from the stela of Khuiuisebek that a *šms.w nj hq3* was in charge of 60 men. This number seems a realistic estimate for the small garrison at Askut.

Besides the military there are two other main branches recorded in Middle Kingdom fortresses: administrators and those in the service sector. For the latter we know for instance about the *jrj-ˁ.t nj ˁ.t hnq.t* who was in charge of the kitchen. With respect to titles for priests the usual minor ranks are attested: *hm-k3, wˁb, hm-ntr, hrj-hb.t, jtj-ntr*.

The question remains, did a transfer to a Nubian fortress imply a setback in a soldier's career or was it seen as a professional promotion?

There is no simple answer to this question, as no information exists about the military career of soldiers garrisoned in Nubia. However, there is no evidence for large-scale Egyptian cemeteries in the vicinity of fortresses in the 12th Dynasty and it therefore seems likely that soldiers only served in Nubia for a short period, returning to and thus being buried in Egypt. Things changed in the 13th Dynasty, when there is evidence of a civilian Egyptian population living together with the soldiers, who were stationed there permanently. The cemeteries where they were buried have been found.

THE SITES IN WAR

The archaeological record offers evidence of the operational history at the described sites only rarely. The few destruction layers we are aware of most likely date back to later periods. However, some missiles made of clay thrown at the enemy who made it as far as the ditch of Buhen have been found.

Although the archaeological evidence is limited, epigraphic sources illustrate that the fortresses indeed played their part in Egyptian campaigns against the enemies further in the south. A few examples are given here.

An inscription of year 19 of King Senusret III was found on the quay of the fortress of Uronarti. It details the last known campaign of the reign of Senusret III. The inscription tells us that – due to the unpleasant time of the year (4th month of Akhet, day 2 = October/November) – war ships got into trouble on their way back. They could no longer navigate on their own and had to be pulled through the dangerous cataract, or, more likely, had to bypass the area on land via a slipway made of mud moistened with water beforehand. A similar installation slipway has been found at Mirgissa.

The text reads:

1) Year 19, fourth month of summer, day 2, under the Majesty of the king of Upper and Lower Egypt, Khakaure (Senusret III), living forever and ever.

2) Having overthrown vile Kush, the Lord, may he live, prosper, and be healthy, proceeded to go downstream.

3) Water (needed to) be found to outdistance Semyak, to go through (the rapids)

4) At the season and all the shoals likewise. As for <…>, it was turbulent,

5) Difficult water indeed to outdistance, to pass through it in this season.

Another inscription detailing an operation has been found at Kumma (Rock Inscription Kumma Number 499 = RIK 116). This inscription belongs to a high official from Kumma who lived under Amenemhet III.

1. Year 9 under his majesty Ni-maat-Ra, who might live until the djet and nechech-eternity.

2. The true friend of the king, his beloved, the judge and mouth of Nechen, Za-mentschu, lord/master of venerability.

3. Everyone, who might pass by this stela and want to reach his home being intact and his wife

4. Being happy. Who wants to embrace his relatives he should say: bread, beer, beef

5. Poultry and an offering that the king makes for Anubis, for the Ka of the judge and mouth of Nechen, born by

6. Zat-ipi, the blessed. I sailed downstreams with my troop without a deceased among (it) in the land of Nubia. I did send nobody to jail but I destroyed and slew the rebels of him for his praise to the king who wishes the right.

This inscription refers to riots in the north of Kumma. The scene of this action seems to have fallen into the responsibility of Za-mentschu, who led a frontier patrol from Kumma which was, of course, successful.

The Semna dispatches

Additional information about frontier patrols can be found in the Semna dispatches, which were written in the reign of Amenemhet III (1856–1803 BC). These are copies of a series of dispatches originating from the Semna and other forts that were compiled in the form of a report on a papyrus. It was found along with other papyri in a Middle Kingdom tomb under the Ramesseum at Thebes in 1896 (now kept in the British Museum, EA 10752). These letters reveal an elaborate communication system among the Nubian fortresses and their central administration, the office of the vizier in Thebes.

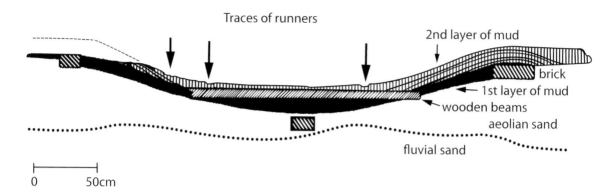

Level of sand before excavating

Traces of runners

2nd layer of mud

brick

1st layer of mud

wooden beams

aeolian sand

fluvial sand

0   50cm

The mud-built slipway at Mirgissa is one of the most fascinating discoveries made during the UNESCO salvage campaign in Nubia. French archaeologists traced the feature over a distance of around 2km (1 mile). The slipway was used to bypass the second cataract when it was not navigable. Ships and goods were hauled on sledges drawn by oxen whose hoofprints were still visible during the excavations, bearing witness to the slipway's last users. Based on A. Vila, in J. Vercoutter (ed.), *Mirgissa I*, Paris, 1970, p. 209, fig. 16.

In particular, they record the arrival and departure of various groups of Nubians, and include the reports of various observation parties who were tracking these hostile forces in the desert.

We are lucky that the Egyptian tendency to elaborate bureaucracy resulted in the reports such as the one quoted below:

Another dispatch brought to him, being the one brought from the dispute overseer Sobekwer, who is in Iken [the ancient Egyptian name for Mirgissa], as one fortress sends a communication to another fortress. It is a communication to you, (may he live, be prosperous, and healthy = lph) to the effect that the two warriors and seventy (?) Medjay-people who had departed following that track in the fourth month of the second season, day four, returned to report to me on the same day at the evening time, bringing three Medjay-men, and four male and female infants(?), saying, 'We found them on the south of the desert margin beneath the inscription of the summer season, and also three women(?),' so they said. I then questioned these Medjay-people, asking, 'From where have you come' Then they replied, 'It's from the well of the region of Ibhayet [south-east of the second cataract] that we have come'.

(...) the (...in) the fourth month of the second season, (day...) came to report (to...). he said concerning (...), 'I departed upon the (track...) explained(?) (...) the (...) brought him (...) the frontier patrol. Then I returned (...,' so he said). I sent word about them to the fortresses that lie north.

(All business affairs of the King's) establishment, life, prosperity, health, are prosperous and flourishing, and all business affairs of yours, (l.p.h, are prosperous and flourishing). It is good if you, l.p.h., take note.

Papyrus, British Museum, EA 10752, recto 2–3

The detailed description of this event reveals one of the main tasks of the soldiers garrisoned in Nubia: to monitor the movement of people carefully and control trading activities in the vicinity of their fortress. Frontier patrols, the so-called *pechert*, were despatched to carry out this task. In this most interesting case Nubian natives, the Medjai, are used as a mercenary force reporting about their own people.

In addition, we learn that neighbouring fortresses had to be informed immediately, as well as the central administration. Thus we have two reporting systems that should have guaranteed total control over the region.

Storming the fortress – insights from pictorial and textual evidence

In order to compensate for the lack of archaeological evidence we face in Middle Kingdom Nubia with respect to how the sites were involved in war, we should investigate one of the most important sources for the study of operational history – the group of scenes that depict the storming of fortresses. A close look at these selected narrative tomb and temple scenes enriches our understanding of the ancient Egyptian fortification system. It is from the way that the Egyptians presented themselves in storming scenes that we are able to draw further conclusions about how they used both offensive and defensive weapon and details about their assault tactics.

Moreover, the illustrations provide us with hints of how the Egyptian military experience in siege warfare had an effect on the way the architects planned and strengthened their fortifications.

A remarkable example comes from the tomb of the general Intef at Thebes, which dates to the 11th Dynasty. The Egyptian soldiers are shown in two registers, equipped with a combination of bows and arrows, battleaxes, spears, daggers and shields. Their target, an Asiatic fortress, can be easily identified by the appearance of the soldiers defending the walls. Besides their typical hairstyle and goatees, it is their small and concave shields that reveals their Asiatic origin. The Egyptians are shown in two registers marching against the fortress; they are also using a mobile siege tower in order to overcome the high walls. A couple of soldiers have already climbed up and successfully clambered over the battlements; their Asiatic opponents are depicted falling from the walls.

Regardless of how small the historical value of such scenes might be, it goes without saying that the experience the Egyptian soldiers made in attacks like the one decribed above resulted in technological innovations. Thus, it does not come as a surprise that only a few decades later new elements to complicate possible assaults were incorporated in Egyptian fortification systems, especially in Nubia.

The dry ditch came into use in order to make attacks using mobile towers and battering rams more difficult. Walls were built higher and broader, gates were strengthened and additional towers were built to increase the potential for flanking fire.

AFTERMATH

By the time of the Second Intermediate Period and the New Kingdom (1780–1070 BC) the fortresses of the Middle Kingdom to the south had lost their significance and been transformed into less fortified cult centres. The new border was pushed further to the south, protected by less fortified fortress towns missing the elaborate fortified nature of their predecessors.

In the northern delta foreigners from Canaan, the Hyksos (princes of foreign countries) established their capital at the fortified city of Avaris/Tell el Daba. Their arrival coincided with the introduction of the horse and chariot, which had not been seen in Egypt before. The Hyksos were also military trained and had better weapons like the sickle sword and more powerful bows.

The answer of the Egyptians to this new power in the north-east was the adaption and the improvement of their weapons and military architecture. New fortresses were built between the north-eastern delta and Gaza via North Sinai to serve as supply bases for the Egyptian army. In Canaan itself

ABOVE

Siege scene from the tomb of General Intef. The archaeological record offers only sparse evidence of sieges in Egyptian history. We nevertheless know from other sources that Egyptian soldiers were experienced in this kind of warfare. In the early Middle Kingdom, representations of siege warfare are found quite frequently. As pharaonic ideology generally demanded the representation of a successful Egyptian army and a likewise defeated enemy, the true outcome of the encounters shown remains unproven. This wall painting from the tomb of General Intef therefore shows a naturally successful attack on an Asiatic fortress. Thebes, 11th Dynasty. (© W. Ruhm, reproduced by courtesy of the German Archaeological Institute, Cairo)

LEFT

Siege scene from the tomb of General Intef, detail. This detail from the siege scene described above shows Egyptian soldiers using a mobile siege tower to attack an Asiatic fortress. (© W. Schiele, reproduced by courtesy of the German Archaeological Institute, Cairo)

governors' residences were built to establish a network of control in foreign territory. The military architecture of the New Kingdom shows many changes, with the internal layouts altered to suit the new realities.

THE SITES TODAY

For those interested in visiting the remains of the Egyptian fortifications introduced here some information should be provided. First of all one should be aware that in many cases there is nothing more to be seen on site than some low mud-brick walls protruding from the dust and sand of the desert.

At the vast majority of sites no one knows anything about the features a well-prepared visitor is looking for. Below is a list of some of the sites worth going to.

National Military Museum, Cairo

The collection of the National Military Museum of Egypt, situated at the Citadel in Cairo, seeks to shed light on the country's military development through all historical periods. The pharaonic collection, which mainly contains reproductions and dioramas, is almost unknown to scholars and the broader public but nevertheless worth a visit. You need to ask the curator to open the more often than not closed wing. Opening hours need to be checked in advance.

Fortified settlement at Ayn Asil, Dakhla Oasis

At Ayn Asil French archaeologists are investigating a fortified settlement with various building phases, dated to the Old Kingdom. For those on a tour through the Western Oasis of Egypt it would be worth asking one of the hotels in Dakhla for a four-wheel-drive car and a driver to discover the spot. As the ancient site is located in the desert the car should be suitable for off-road driving.

Aswan, Elephantine

Remains of Egypt's oldest known fortress discovered on Elephantine Island can be visited easily, as the impressive walls are a stop on the official circular walk of the site.

The National Military Museum, Cairo. The pharaonic collection of the National Military Museum of Egypt, situated at the Citadel in Cairo, is small and unheralded. However, enthusiastic visitors are welcome and will be impressed by the coverage of the period. (© M. Reinemer)

Ayn Asil, entrance to the Ka-chapel of the governor of the oasis, Medu-nefer. The ruler of the isolated fortified town at Ayn Asil in the Dakhla oasis, officially claimed as 'rulers of the desert', were worshipped by later generations who built them individual chapels next to their former area of influence.

For opening hours consult the website of the German Archaeological Institute, Cairo, in advance.

The last traces of the protective wall to the south-east of modern Aswan are more difficult to discover. The first visible remains start somewhere south of the Islamic cemetery, which is situated to the east of the garden of the Nubian Museum. The best-preserved part of the wall still stands to the north of the old dam near Shellal. Modern military camps are located in the region and walking close to these installations is not allowed.

The National Museum, Khartoum. The National Museum in Khartoum houses a huge collection of Nubian antiquities. Among them are many items originating from Middle Kingdom fortresses.

Shalfak and Uronarti

These two mud-brick fortresses in the region of the former second cataract are situated in the middle of nowhere. Access to those spots demands at the very least a small boat. For the time being the only reasonable way to see the site is through participation in a guided, but highly individual tour of Sudan. Occassionally agencies include the sites in their tour programmes and the option needs to be checked with the specialist travel agencies.

Khartoum, National Museum

A large number of objects discovered in the chain of Nubian fortresses are spread throughout museums all over the world, but a special collection worth mentioning is on display in the National Museum of Khartoum. During the Nubian salvage campaigns entire temples were dismantled and transported to Sudan's capital where they found a new home in the garden of the National Museum. Of special interest are the temples from Buhen, Semna-West and Kumma. Various rock inscriptions found in the area of the Nubian fortresses were removed and installed here.

FURTHER READING

Adams, W. Y., *Nubia: Corridor to Africa* Princeton, 1977
—, 'The First Colonial Empire: Egypt in Nubia, 3200–1200 BC', *Comparative Studies in Society and History* Vol. 26, No. 1 (Jan., 1984), pp. 36–71

Badawy, A., *A Preliminary Report on the Excavations by the University of California at Askut. First Season October 1962–January 1963*, *Kush 12*, 1964, pp. 47–53

Bonnet, C., 'The Kerma Culture', in Welsby, D., and Anderson, J. R. (eds.), *Sudan – Ancient Treasures. An exhibition of recent discoveries from the Sudan National Museum* London, 2004, pp. 70–82

Borchardt, L., *Altägyptische Festungen an der zweiten Nilschnelle* Wiesbaden, 1923

Dunham D., and Janssen, J. M. A., *Second Cataract Forts I. Semna-Kumma* Boston, 1960

Dunham, D. (ed.), *Second Cataract Forts II. Uronarti, Shalfak, Mirgissa* Boston, 1967

Emery, W. B., Smith, H. S., and Millard, A., *The Fortress of Buhen: The Archaeological Report. (Excavations at Buhen) Part 1. 49th Excavation Memoir* London, 1979

Gardiner, A. H., 'An ancient list of the fortresses of Nubia', *JEA 3* 1916, pp. 184–92

Grajetzki, W., *The Middle Kingdom of Ancient Egypt. History, Archaeology and Society* London, 2006

——, 'The Investigation of the Ancient Wall extending from Aswan to Philae. First Preliminary Report', *MDAIK 43*, 1986, pp. 67–74

Jaritz, H., 'The Investigation of the Ancient Wall extending from Aswan to Philae. Second Preliminary Report', *MDAIK 49*, 1993, pp. 108–32

Kemp, B. J., 'Large Middle Kingdom Granary Buildings (and the archaeology of administration)', *ZÄS 113*, 1986, pp. 120–36

——, *Ancient Egypt. Anatomy of a Civilization* 2nd edition, London, New York, 2006

Lawrence, W., 'Ancient Egyptian Fortifications', *JEA 51*, 1965, pp. 69ff.

McDermott, B., *Warfare in ancient Egypt* Thrupp, 2004

Meurer, G., 'Nubier in Ägypten bis zum Beginn des Neuen Reiches: Zur Deutung der Stele 14753' *ADAIK*, Ägyptologische Reihe 13 (Berlin, 1996)

Moorsel, P. van, 'Once more: "Quid novi ex Africa?" (The Non-Phenomena in Nubian Archaeology after Lille, 1994)', *CRIPEL 17*, 1, pp. 61–66

Mumford, G., 'Tell Ras Budran (Site 345): Defining Egypt's Eastern Frontier and Mining Operations in South Sinai during the Late Old Kingdom (Early EB IV/MB I)', *BASOR 342*, 2006, pp. 1–55

——, 'Beyond Egypt's Frontiers: A Late Old Kingdom Fort in South Sinai', *Minerva 16*, 3, 2005, pp. 24–26

Newberry, P. E., *Beni Hasan I* London, 1893

Partridge, R. B., *Fighting Pharaohs: Weapons and Warfare in Ancient Egypt* Manchester, 2002

Śliwa, J., 'Die Siedlung des Mittleren Reiches bei Qasr el-Sagha. Grabungsbericht 1983 und 1985', *MDAIK 42*, 1986, pp. 167–79

——, 'Die Siedlung des Mittleren Reiches bei Qasr el-Sagha. Grabungsbericht 1987 und 1988', *MDAIK 48*, 1992, pp. 177–91

Smith, H. S., *The Fortress of Buhen: Inscriptions, (Excavations at Buhen)* London, 1976

Smith, S. T., 'Askut and the Role of the Second Cataract Forts', *JARCE 28*, 1991, pp. 107–32

——, 'The First Imperialists', *KMT 3.3*, 1992, pp. 40–49, 78–79

——, *Askut in Nubia: the Economics and Ideology of Egyptian Imperialism in the Second Millenium BC* London, New York 1995

——, *Wretched Kush: Ethnic identities and boundaries in Egypt's Nubian Empire* London, New York, 2003

Smither, P. C., 'The Semnah Dispatches', *JEA 31*, 1945, pp. 3–10

Spencer, A. J., *Brick Architecture in Ancient Egypt* Warminster/Wilts Spencer, 1979

Steindorff, G., *Aniba II* Leipzig, 1937

Vercoutter, J., *Mirgissa I* Paris, 1970

Vogel, C., 'Archäologische und epigraphische Belege zur Nilschiffahrt im Bereich des Zweiten Katarakts', *SAK* 26, 1998, pp. 261–272

——, *Ägyptische Festungen und Garnisonen bis zum Ende des Mittleren Reiches.* Hildesheimer ägyptologische Beiträge, 46 (Hildesheim, 2004)

——, *Master Architects of Ancient Nubia: Space-saving solutions in Middle Kingdom Fortresses*, in prep.

——, 'Storming the gates? Entrance protection in the military architecture of Middle Kingdom Nubia', in M. Bietak, E. Czerny, I. Forstner-Müller (eds.), *Cities and urbanism in Ancient Egypt: Papers from a workshop in November 2006 at the Austrian Academy of Sciences*, Österreichische Akademie der Wissenschaften Denkschriften der Gesamtakademie LX, Untersuchungen der Zweigstelle Kairo des Österreichischen Archäologischen Institutes XXXV, Wien, pp. 299–320

Welsby, D., 'Ancient Treasures of Lake Nubia', *Sudan & Nubia Bulletin* 8, 2004, pp. 103–04

Žába, Z., Hintze, F., and Verner, M., *The Rock inscriptions of Lower Nubia (Czechoslovak concession)* Czechoslovak Institute of Egyptology in Prague and in Cairo Publications, Volume I: Prague, 1974

GLOSSARY

Egyptological terms
Old Kingdom

The chronology of Pharaonic Egypt is subdivided into three main periods of time: Old, Middle and New Kingdom. The Old Kingdom follows the Early Dynastic Period and covers the period *c.*2613–2181 BC. Three important fortifications were built within this time frame: a fortified settlement on Elephantine island, the fortified governor's residences at Ayn Asil, Dakhla Oasis, and the round fortress of Ras Budran in the Sinai Peninsula.

Middle Kingdom

With respect to military architecture the Egyptian Middle Kingdom (2040–1782 BC) can be considerd as the country's Golden Age. After a troublesome period of inner conflicts (known as the First Intermediate Period) the Theban king Mentuhotep II was able to reunite the two separate kingdoms based on Herakleopolis and Thebes. The renewed state took advantage of its consolidated power and directed its energy southwards. Some reigns later, Senusret I, initiated the building of various fortifications in Lower Nubia, among them the famous site of Buhen.

Technical terms (mainly after Stephen Francis Wyley)

Battlement	The upper part of a fortifications wall from which defenders defended their position. The battlement, or parapet, was usually provided with crenels and merlons; the crenels were the openings and the merlons were the solid uprights. This arrangement allowed the defenders to fire upon attackers through the crenels while obtaining some protection from the returned enemy fire behind the merlons.
Berm	A narrow path running between the ditch and the parapet.

Counterscarp	The outer side of a ditch, in some permanent fortifications it was faced with stone to make entering and retreating from the ditch more dangerous.
Crenels	Part of the parapet that is intended to alternate with the upright merlons.
Crenellated	Fortified or provided with crenels. In Old and Middle Kingdom Egypt crenels are known by iconographical evidence only. However, later buildings such as the fortified temple walls of Medinet Habu possess them and make it likely for earlier periods as well.
Escarp/scarp	The side of the ditch next to the parapet.
Glacis	The area outside the ditch which was scarped into a gentle slope running downwards from the covered way towards the open country, which was kept deliberately free of any form of cover.
Loopholes	A narrow opening in the wall of a fortification, through which missiles were discharged at the enemy.
Merlons	(1) The portion of a battlemented parapet that rises up from a wall (eg. the solid part of a parapet between the crenels). (2) The part of a parapet between two embrasures.
Moat/ditch	Usually cut into the rock in front of the main wall and varying in depth and width. A common feature for Middle Kingdom fortresses in Nubia.
Parapet	The top of a wall of either a fortification or fieldwork, either plain or battlemented. Used to provide protection for the defenders behind the wall.
Rampart	An enbankment of earth used for the purpose of defence, excavated from the ditch and either raised on the inside or outside of the ditch. The simplest method of constructing a rampart was by excavating a ditch and casting the soil inwards to form a 'dump'. This was often reinforced by a wall or palisade along the top.

INDEX

References to illustrations are shown in **bold**. Plates are prefixed pl, with captions on the page in brackets.